W9-BFT-001

Unmasking the Lie

Unmasking the Lie
Exploring the
Wonders of Forgiveness

Anthony Lobo

Copyright © 2010 The Bombay Saint Paul Society

ISBN 978-81-7108-726-6

Cover: Manoj Pal

Title: Audrey D'Mello

2nd Print February 2012

Contact:
Editorial: editorsp@gmail.com
Marketing: stpaulsmarketing@gmail.com
Website: www.stpaulsbyb.com

Printed by Jose Paul at St Paul Press Training School,
Nagasandra, Bengaluru and published
by BETTER YOURSELF BOOKS,
58/23rd Road, TPS III, Bandra, Mumbai– 400 050
2012

Contents

Dedication

This work is dedicated to my wife Christina,
without whom it would never have been possible.
She has been my right hand all along
and if I may add, my right leg too!
This work is also dedicated to our six children
we describe as our three 'biggies'
and our three 'smallies',
who have taught me much about sacrifice,
acceptance, communication, laughter and forgivness.

Foreword

Franklin my brother has been friend and philosopher. Along with Christina, the three of us have made a great team.

Appreciation and gratitude to Hilary Miranda s.j.,(late) who has been over the years, mentor and guide. Ever grateful thanks too, to the team who made these healing programmes possible: Eugenie deSousa, Odette Gonsalves, Zita D'Mello, Ian and Audrey D'Mello and my brother/sister of long standing, Ralph and Doreen Fernandes.

Finally, sincere thanks to a dear friend, Mary Usha SND, who first lead me into this experience of inner healing, whose pupil I am proud to be and who will always hold a special place in my heart. She is the one who first initiated the Forgiveness Therapy.

Introduction

A locally produced stage play titled FIRE AND BRIMSTONE, a hilarious depiction of the ministrations of the devil in a local Church fellowship, had this banner as one of its stage props.

BECOME GOD
Quick and easy lessons. Invitation to all.

Sly and provocative no doubt. A deception? Or could there be a grain of truth in what it claimed to achieve. Faced squarely with this invitation, some in their simplicity and ignorance might readily jump to it, affirming their desire to accept. Perhaps they might even get their cue from movies such as "Bruce Almighty".

Others more of the religious kind might abhor such an invitation as being in poor taste, a delusion, derogatory to religious beliefs. They would be content, living out their human life as best as possible and in humility.

Then there are those who would answer emphatically in the negative, believing they are living free from religious bigotry, spiritual fears and social norms. Yet unknown to themselves, they live a life of deception. They least realize how in their own individual ways, they take on the role of God, becoming an absolute power in themselves.

Who therefore is God? What is the general concept and understanding of who God is? For many, God is maker and creator of all things. He is all powerful, almighty, all knowing and all seeing. He controls the heavens and the galaxies in space. He gives life and takes it away.

From this proceeds the belief that God is person, a Divine Being who loves and relates deeply enough to take care of their every need. He makes personal contact and communication possible. He provides, protects and multiplies. He has a plan and purpose for all human kind.

Others are not sure which way He might lean and depend upon His ultimate mercy. He gives sickness and suffering, allows poverty and disaster, death and destruction. Fear of God is what governs their action, their motivation, their decisions and their lives.

Many would rather have an understanding of Him without the help of any particular religion or creed. For some, human life and suffering is a matter of destiny or fate. Others prefer to conceive of God, not as 'person' but a 'nebulous force' up there in the sky. God is something if not someone, to be respected, feared, contended with. An all-pervading Being.

Still others, feel comfortable with themselves as long as they have some concern for nature, for animals, the poor and disaster victims. This they do by attaching their name to financial contributions, aids and charities. They do not want or need a God who will interfere in their personal lives.

Then there is the growing idea emanating from New Age philosophies that 'God is all and all is God'. God, according to this thought pattern is not person but an energy that exists in all beings and things, that encompasses all, an energy that is sufficient to handle every need that man might require.

Finally there are those who do not want to believe in His existence.

Yet for the majority, God is Free, Independent, Sovereign and an All-powerful Divine Person. No one dictates to Him. He thinks, feels and does; as he wants, how he wants and whenever he wants. He thinks best. He knows best. He decides for himself. He is the author of life. He takes it away as and when.

But what happens when a person chooses not to listen to what this God desires or directs but rather prefers to do his own thing. Does such a person become a god unto himself?

10

A little child is disobedient and robustly insists on its own way. Could this be the early beginnings of becoming an authority to itself. If allowed to go unchecked, will it/he not in his later years, become an all demanding and all expecting Lord. When he decides that belief in God is manipulative; praying to this God is farcical; trusting in this God's protection and provision, displays weakness of character; and therefore begins to trust only in himself, his talents, his decisions and intelligence – Is he becoming a sovereign and independent entity?

He decides that his freedom and happiness is all that matters. He decides that he has the right to find them in any method he so chooses. This might mean living in free and temporary relationships, or attempting to develop a family with persons of the same sex, or doing away with foetus' and aged persons when inconvenient. By thus rejecting every social norm built up over the centuries, is he aiming to become a "no one can touch me" power to himself?

Is he saying to himself and the world "my rules are my own and I can change them at will. I decide when to give life and when to take it away. I have my own approach to sexuality; my personal philosophy of life, its meaning and purpose. And well, the devastating psychological implications upon persons in each of the above situations – I declare that they no longer exist".

As a young lad, at my very first visit to the U.S.A., one remark lay imprinted upon my memory – "Over here you have the freedom to do what you want, to be what you want" – Man's actions, his thoughts, his theories, his beliefs may go against normal patterns of society, religious beliefs and social concerns.

But what is most important is himself. His freedom comes first. His rights transcend everything else. "This is my life. This is my body. This is my soul. I can do whatever I want or choose. No one can tell me what I can do and what I cannot do. I am the master of my life and my destiny". If this is not becoming god, what is?

Emblazoned upon a T shirt was this caption:

I THOUGHT I WAS AN ATHEIST,
UNTIL I REALIZED I WAS GOD

An atheist is one who does not believe in the existence of God. How could he, if he is the only god in existence. Therefore he believes only in himself.

Is this a sign therefore of man's own inner self, independence and freedom, rising up to become absolute and unquestionable. Is this a symbol of rebellion; rebellion against any authority and power over himself. A rebellion therefore against any spiritual force or influence telling him how he should conduct his life. A rebellion against not only society, cultures and traditions but against the very initiator of life., i.e. God Himself?

Faith is losing ground. Faith in others and especially faith in God, is of no consequence. The in-thing now is Intellectualism. Intellectualizing of life, its beginnings and purpose. Intellectualizing the mysteries of science, tsunamis and the infinity of space. Finally, the intellectualizing of God himself. Hence *if God is acknowledged, he has to exist and be, on pre-determined terms and conditions.*

Man's intellect has reached peaks of refinement and specialization. He has grown so used to "thinking" and "reasoning out", that he has fallen in love with his intelligence, with his capabilities, with himself. Nothing else and no one else is important. He alone is what counts. He alone, is of sole importance.

No wonder then that, he is attracted by modern philosophies, new age gurus, meditation techniques and even satanic rituals that teach him, I am god. Not that God dwells in him, but that he is god. All he needs to do is go through a process of shedding his earthliness and human weakness so that the god he is, can emerge stronger and prominent.

In believing and behaving as god, he feels good about himself. He feels a satisfaction from deep within. He feels a sense of self-realization, self-attainment and nirvana.

Could this be the ENLIGHTENMENT
he has been searching for?
OR
Is this the epitome of PRIDE
and ARROGANCE and DECEPTION?

It is becoming more popular for people, despite their education, despite their religious affiliations, despite their cultural backgrounds; to be influenced by these philosophies. And it is also becoming popular for Corporate and Business houses to join this band-wagon using this concept, in order to sell their wares.

Announcing a performance of a legendary guitarist:

...Meet the God of Guitar. Add one more name to your list of gods. Be there to worship him...

...Sell your soul to the devil and get a pizza that will fulfill your every need...

What then is the driving force behind this independence, this desire for freedom, this authority that he loves to wield. Is it purely of an intelligent nature, emanating from reason and argument. Is it a result of intensive deliberation of the mysteries of the universe and man. Does it proceed from long years of study and research. Is it a product of scientific fact-finding and mathematics?

Or does it spring from a deep down need in the feelings and emotions of man. Does it speak of a longing for self-actualization, self-satisfaction and fulfillment; a hunger to be heeded and respected; to feel good about himself, a thirsting to be accepted and loved. Does it speak of the need to be recognized, appreciated and cherished for who he is and needs to be?

This then is an attempt to analyze and understand the greatest innermost thrusts and desires that compels him to believe and do what he does. In so doing, a story of intrigue and deceit begins to unfold. A story that reveals to us, what exactly governs, directs, influences the man of today. What really makes him 'tick'. And I trust that each one who might read this book will find a slot for himself/herself, will find understanding to the life he/she has chosen, will find a pathway to peace and happiness.

What is attempted here is:

i)   an analysis of negativity that deep emotional root hurts cause.

ii) an eraser or healing of the same.

iii) an attempt to realize and restore man's basic goodness, character, virtue and higher calling.

I believe that the content of this book applies to all peoples and nations, irrespective of caste or creed, culture or society, colour or race. No one is exempt. Examples and testimonies, illustrations and characters highlighted, have been used in order to draw out crucial emotional and human principles this book speaks of. Psychological principles applied, are recognized as standard truths, having been well established and utilized for many years now.

Examples: Moses of 'The Ten Commandments' movie fame, was an example of an unusual spiritual leader. He faced the onslaught of evil represented by the Egyptian King, with a faith in God, unknown to any man. Yet it might come as a surprise to many, that he had a 'fear' ingrained into his personality, powerful enough to destroy him.

OR

Zacchaeus, short and stunted and yet with a terrific ambition and zest for power. What was the secret hidden within his character to make him such?

OR

What drove men of history, like Napolean and Hitler to become symbols of fear and tyranny?

In attempting to explain these basic principles, cause and effect; repetition of phrases, words and ideas become essential.

14

The key is to find your place; to find that, that fits you; to apply the principles and the conclusions drawn; so that a more comprehensive understanding of the self becomes possible.

Numbered examples are real life experiences of people, whose names have been changed for reasons of confidentiality.

Finally, discussing characters and quotations from the Bible and explaining Forgiveness from a secular and Christian perspective is not to be understood as an attempt to proselytize. The only objective is to provide the fuller and more complete benefits of forgiveness, for the good of all.

Chapter One

KALEIDESCOPE

Sex, sex and again sex. Give me, give me more. Do it with others. Can't get enough.

Emptiness gnawing at the heart. Loneliness driving me crazy.

Pornography and paedophilia. Blue movies. Alcohol and drugs.

The cry goes on.

Searching, thirsting, groping, hungering. Nobody understands. Nobody is listening.

Ova is released. Sperm hurtling down to fuse together. Life is conceived. Miracle of miracles.

Halt! Is it convenient? It's not the right time. Other plans in the making. Cut it out. Tear it out.

My choice. My life. My body. Blame it on the other.

Baby is born. Love, love, love. Photographs. Video. Cooey, cooey. Baby clothes.

Blue is for boys, pink is for girls. Toys, dolls and steam engines. How gorgeous.

Rooting for a boy. No, rather prefer a girl. Never perfect. Always something missing.

Blame it on the genes. Blame it on the wife.

Back to work. Crèches. Baby sitters. Rejection. Loneliness. Where is mom?

Where is dad? Hi! baby, bye baby. Got no time. Must make the bread.

Where has love gone? Don't want the feeding bottle.

Only want mother's breast, mother's heartbeat, mother's comfort.

Hurting Childhood. Comparisons. High expectations. Belittling. Ridicule. Careers.

Mum and dad quarrelling. Differences. Late nights. Other affairs. Fights.

Divorce. Because they love me so much. Court controlled visits. A new dad? A new mum?

Hate. Anger. Violence. Drugs. Rock music. Fast cars. Gambling. Stealing.

Hooky from school. Run away from home. Where to turn? Whom to turn to?

Girl friends. Boy friends. Dating and more. Smooching. Caressing. Let's just do it man.

Or be left out. Sweet sixteen. I want to be a virgin. Yuck, you silly thing. Prude. Peer group.

Sex. Everybody's doing it. Your body man. Enjoy it. Experiment. Making out.

In school. In the car. In the basement. Same sex.

No fear of dad. No fear of God. Law is behind me.

Marry at seventeen. Run away from nagging mom, tyrant dad.

Run into the arms of my true love. Finally, somebody who really cares.

I feel so good. I feel so protected. I feel so secure.

Forget the past. Break free from painful memories that haunt and bind. Marriage solves all.

Or will it? Why marry? Co-habitation is the hep thing. No commitments. No legal tangles.

Give it a try. Have a baby and see how it works. Be free. No hassles.

Do your own thing. Your life. Your time. Your future.

Infidelity. After children. After grand children! Emptiness gnawing once again.

Yearnings. Urges. Roving eyes. Buxom blondes.

Unfaithful spouses. Marriage breaks up. In three months. In one year. After twenty years.

Simple folk and Intellectuals.

Professionals and politicians.

Royalty.

Presidents and Kings.

Preachers too.

The search is on. Hungering for satisfaction. Thirsting for peace. Yearning for love.

Chapter Two

THE SPIDER'S WEB

Sadly this is the trend; the norm for life, for our society and civilization. Families are no longer able to hold together. Couples no longer know how to cope, how to relate, how to love. Sex is the attractive factor. Sex in all its forms, colours and perversities. Sex is the instrument used for "making out" rather than "building a relationship of love".

The meaning of communication; the importance of forgiveness; the call to sacrifice and steadfastness in committed relationships; is forgotten and lost. Children as a result are unable to find security at home and look for it in so many attractions.

The focus has shifted from family and community, from togetherness and the other; to the self, self-assertion and realization, independence and freedom.

Each one gives his/her own reasons and explanations for values, behaviour and actions. Norms that were acceptable for family, for religious beliefs and for society are no longer acceptable. Yet road rules, traffic rules, recreational safety rules are adhered to strictly, punishable by fine or otherwise.

While he does not have to adhere to religious rules or regulations or guidelines for living life, he dashed well adhere to the rules of the country. Hence while penal laws have to be adhered to, spiritual laws can be easily dispensed with.

Where then is man headed for. Why so much brokenness. Why end up piling hurt upon hurt, pain over pain, especially to those nearest and dearest to him. The pleasure of healthy sex does not seem to meet his needs. Family and children fall far short of satiating him. And yet, Divorce all but kills him. Drowning himself in work, alcohol, golf and the rest, only maintains an artificial peace. What does he hope to gain. What is he aiming to achieve?

His Phenomenal Intelligence...

The development and progress made during this last century has been phenomenal. The things we are able to do today in science and medicine; the confidence with which we are able to reach into outer space and the depths of our oceans; the progress in technology, electronics and the micro chip; the ability to shrink the size of the world through communications, information technology and the internet; the study of DNA and stem cell research; can only speak of the phenomenal intelligence of man and of his great capabilities.

As Against Family And Relationships...

But what good is all of this if man himself remains broken and miserable within himself. What is the use of such tremendous advancement, if he has not yet been able to travel the short distance into his own heart and meet the incessant cry of his inner spirit? Despite the scientific and technological progress he has made over the years, he remains an utter failure.

For, he is not able to live in peace and harmony with even a single person, his life's partner, for the length of his life. His marriage has broken up; his children have been wrestled away from him and he can see them only by appointment.

Whereas the only thing they really need is security. A security that comes from a home, which withstands the test of conflict and struggle. A security which he can no longer provide.

Instead they receive an inheritance of loneliness, rage, guilt and fear. They too multiply in God's plan and pass on this same broken-ness to the generations:

- Divorce and separation has become an every day affair; a prerogative not of the poor and illiterate but instead of the educated and modern intellectual.

- The Marriage Agreement has been reduced to the level of a "Partnership at Will". Not forgetting the pre-nuptial agreement to safeguard one and all! The partnership remains intact as long as confidences remain. But when things get a bit sticky and the partners are no longer comfortable with each other, they decide to go their separate ways.

Unfortunately, the products of marriage i.e. the children; cannot be sub-divided like the assets of the partnership. They turn sour, they tend to rust and disintegrate, they bend out of alignment and even break. No wonder then:

- Children torture and even put to death other siblings and contemporaries.
- Teenagers reputed to come from good homes, go on a rampage gunning down other students.
- Others hacking to death their grand-mothers on some paltry disagreement.
- Thirteen year olds barely able to write an essay, attending class pregnant with child.
- Eighty percent of boys, by the time they enter their teens, have seen a blue movie.
- People being robbed and murdered for the sake of their fancy sports shoes. Others being driven to suicide for lack of the same.
- Prejudices against race, religion, sects and color.
- Prostitution, child sex, homosexuality, single parents, rape and incest, wife battering and child abuse, abortion, euthanasia, female infanticide, each in its own way trying to satiate that inner need.
- Not only parents filing suit against one another for custody of their children; but children taking parents to court.
- Teen sex on the rampage and even encouraged. To prevent the spread of AIDS, boys are freely given condoms and girls pregnancy kits.

Example 1: Angela

Angela's first day of work in her new job with a multi-national, left her stunned and shaken. Her boss, a woman, was a true example of a shrew, which until then she had only read about ! She had the highest expectations of Angela, regularly yelled and screamed at her, made new demands by the minute, changed her instructions at every alternative one, swore and used abusive language. The reason the company kept her on was due to the fact she was the best in her field and in great demand by their offices the world over.

By the end of her first week in her new job, Angela was all set to pack in the towel. Having approached me about the situation, I surmised there was some great distress in the boss's life, for her to behave in such a manner. It turned out that she was a divorcee. This meant that on the one hand she (Angela's Boss) was an expert in her field, excellent in her work, a perfectionist, extremely able and capable and therefore a great asset to the company.

On the other hand she was a failure in home matters, in her marriage and personal relationships. She would take out her frustration on poor Angela. But with counsel and advice Angela was not only able to overcome her fear and dislike of her boss but was soon able to stand up to her and speak plainly to her about her attitudes.

Angela turned out to be the only secretary in the whole organization (young and in her first major job) that stuck it out with the lady without complaining once to Personnel. Later when this boss was transferred to a new office, her first choice for secretary, was Angela. This turn about took place because Angela had grown into a new awareness of herself and her identity, by dealing with past and unresolved issues; leading to a growth in security and self-confidence. The boss on the other hand had not the opportunity or guidance to look into herself, to know and love herself for who she was; but instead merely gave in to frustration and guilt of her failed relationships.

23

The difficulties involved and humility required to maintain a marriage relationship and family security, is asking too much for modern man. I know of a young man of Asian descent, living and working in Europe, who finally called off a friendship with a young lady because she could not conceive in her mind the idea that, marriage could ever be for life. My freedom is at stake no matter if it costs the children's happiness. Perhaps this is why we'd rather not have children, but abort them instead.

To avoid divorce proceedings, law suits for alimony and division of property; we'd rather not get married. A new kind of living arrangement would be easier on all. No commitment, no exchange of rings, no sharing of income and wealth, no children, no taking care of aged parents. In other words; no love, no sacrifice, no acceptance and sharing of hardships and pain. Just raw passion, sex, friendships.

Then there are those children who are born not out of wedlock but casual relationships and surrogate mothers. The stigma and emotional battering scarring them as a result is never contemplated or understood. Cloning and finally the Lesbian woman "fathering" her child is the "enlightened right" of the day for some; the height of absurdity to others. Children are expected to become full and contributing members of society without biological parents, with foster parents, having emerged from test tubes – one of their homosexual parents having paid for the germination of his sperm with a stranger's egg.

God is lost somewhere in the middle of this new life style; devil worship and satanic rituals have taken His place.

Is this the legacy we leave behind for our children and grand-children. Can we be truly proud of our behaviour and such accomplishments. Can this be considered a progressive society? Because he is no longer able to keep his family together, because he is unwilling to take responsibility for what he has begun; he takes the easy way out, he rationalizes alternative forms of behaviour and relationships.

The institution of Marriage coming down through the ages and accepted and followed by practically every race, religion, nomadic and jungle tribe; is slowly yet stubbornly being corrupted and destroyed. Marriage is the nucleus of a people, a culture, a race, a nation. Destroy it and you are left with nothing.

Thus it would seem that but for a few exceptions, all that Man is able to accomplish in his personal relationships is leave behind a trail of pain, bitterness and brokenness.

There seems to be an innermost need, an innermost urge and hunger that drives man of today. There is that something at the base of his skull, at the bottom of his heart, in the pit of his belly that has not yet been touched. Something that has been bypassed, despite his hectic activities and relationships.

Without question it is the satisfaction of needs, the fulfillment of desires, the search for peace and contentment. This is the longing and the emotional make up of every man. Man's cry for acceptance and love.

Some try to find it through rare feats of dare-devilry and adventure, others through actions of cruelty and gruesomeness. Most seek it through sexuality and its perversities, making this line of life the multi-billion dollar business it has become. There are those who seek it through money power, the power and authority over others. Finally we have the life of glamour, glistening and lights.

And in every one of these forms the bottom line is the search for acceptance, the cry for appreciation, the thirst for feeling good, worthy and needed.

Where then should his great intelligence and capabilities be focused. What is the best use he could put them to. **Technological innovations** or **family and relationships?** Excelling in both would be the ideal, failing which, what should take precedence. What ought to take top most priority in his life.

This man whose intelligence is far greater than any other living creature; this man who is capable of so much; has penetrated the mysteries of outer space and the depths of micro organisms, brought to life facts that are a million years old, is able to destroy cities and countries with the mere press of a button; is he not meant for higher things. Could he not conduct his personal life with a little more dignity and aplomb. Is he not more superior than animals and flying creatures. Is he therefore not called to live a life in every way more superior to them?

Looking at it through the eyes of Religion and Philosophy, is he not called to a higher moral standard of behaviour, of values and harmonious relationships. Is there not a higher purpose, a higher motivation, a higher vision that he aims for. Created as children of a unique God, is he not expected to lead his life in imitation of that same God?

What therefore is there to stop him from living a life more loving, more caring, more understanding, more sacrificing and finally more committed. It is my hope that you, dear reader, will come to realize that there is a higher call to man. The call to live in peace, in harmony, in unity.

Example 2: Lillian

My Christian faith never made any sense to me as I had never experienced anything promised. Prayer was a disaster as within a few minutes I would be distracted. Also, I always did things to please others.

Reluctantly, I agreed to do the programme and felt like a Kindergarten child who is being dragged to the classroom on the first day of school. I thank God however for the same as it was a beginning of change for me.

The first day went smoothly enough with all the input and instruction. On the second day when I attempted to do the forgiveness therapy, I could not, stopped and refused to try again. No matter how much they encouraged me, I refused to do it. Suddenly I broke down and begged to be allowed to go home. I cried and pleaded like a little child for an hour and more but they refused (I was in no state to travel alone) and instead encouraged me to be quiet, by myself, secluded from the rest of the group. I cried with deep pain and sadness. After calming down I continued with the programme.

The next day I was at peace and smiling. I realized I had to release pent up rage and sadness. At the time when my dad passed away, I was not allowed to cry and therefore had sorrow suppressed deep inside. For reasons, I was even blamed for his death. Though he may not have been the best husband or father, I loved him very dearly and like a little baby had to let go of him.

Lumps on my breasts totally disappeared. Fear of marriage has since left me as I continued to do the therapy. I was filled with Love, Peace and a confidence in myself, I had never known before. I could not stop sharing my experiences with family and friends. I had changed. Mum and brother too seemed to have changed. I have every hope of a good future.

Extracts of a testimony:

Before the programme I was broken down and frustrated. There seemed to be a dead-end because of my illness (life threatening). After counseling and the forgiveness therapy I was transformed so to say, I found my real identity. I believe I will be victorious and my life meaningful.

Chapter Three

MARRIAGE AND COMMITMENT

The Games People Play

Marriage has become a game, a game people like to play every now and then. When they tire of the game, they take a break from their partner and return to life as a single person again. But this time, in many if not all cases, as a 'Single Parent'. But the game does not end. Each one in turn begins a fresh round of the game and so it goes on. They content themselves, for some time at least, with another partner, with other children, while all the time protecting their rights to the children of the first partner.

The children themselves become torn and fragmented, divided in their loyalties, try to live up to the demands and directions of three parents now, try to cope without the love and attention they so desperately need. Whom do they belong to. What is their true identity?

No doubt this concept has become a reality today and will be even more so as the years go by. *But is it at all possible that this concept and understanding of life could have existed from the beginning.* Is it at all possible that this could be part of that 'Higher Calling' to Man that we are dealing with in this book.

Again, marriages of today can be likened to a 'whist drive' where after every game, points are collected and partners are exchanged. The winning duo though ending up at the finishing line almost never began as partners.

Some of the other games people play, are 'wife swapping' at get-togethers for the jet-set and corporate executives. Young couples are known to meet other young couples over the net and exchange partners to learn new ways of satisfying sexual appetites. The idea behind this arrangement is to keep the romance and excitement in marriage with the spouse, strong. It would seem very clearly that in these cases, marriage is merely an excuse, a screen behind which sexual appetites are satisfied.

Imagine two people coming together; in making love and producing a child give tenderly of their hearts, their feelings, their bodies; joining together their intellect, finance and artistic skills to plan and build their home.

Imagine these two people then separating, to follow the cycle all over again with someone else. What similarity does one find with this kind of behavior pattern, elsewhere on this wonderful planet called Earth? Where else except with the other inhabitants of this planet such as the animals and birds. And thus follows the next question, "Is Man merely an animal or has he lowered himself to become and behave like one of them?"

Animal enthusiasts seem to believe that animals are a better species than humans. Animals are sweeter, gentler, more loving and definitely more trustworthy and dependable. Animal rights and animal food is big business. There are those who are also claiming equal rights for animal offspring such as the Chimpanzee, as human children have. And probably there are those who might even prefer to be born again as animals in their next life. The truth of much they claim, cannot be denied. And yet, are human beings the same as animals?

At our home we have always been fond of dogs. On occasion we would have our pet mated with another. That other would belong to someone else. The other animal has never lived together with ours, supported her or encouraged her through the pregnancy and after the pups were born. She would give birth and look after those pups by herself. The pups unlike humans, do not need their father beside them every moment of their life. After a couple of months the pups would be sold. It might cost our dog a few sniffs and a whimper but soon she would be ready for the cycle all over again.

Many thousands of animal lovers have done the same with their animal pets. Those who own Champions, give them out at a fee to mate with and impregnate other bitches with their seed. Ignorant of the connection, man is doing the very same in a less obvious but nevertheless monetary way. He demands the most beautiful and perhaps voluptuous women. She lusts after the more handsome and successful stars. When it is all over they rake in their respective shares of the estate.

By behaving such, is he not reducing his calling, his wonderful existence, his keen intellect and ability to relate, love and understand; to the level of creatures like the animals? We may provide all sorts of modern psychological and philosophical explanations, reasons and excuses for one's behavior and decisions; but in the long run, like it or not, that is exactly what we are doing to the Human Race.

Watching Hollywood movies can be gripping and convincing. The media is immensely powerful. But there is a gap many miles long, between the plot of the story and what actually happens in peoples lives.

One movie for example spoke of this hero who was being sued for sexual harassment. The destruction of his life, his marriage and all he had attained by hard work was imminent. Till at the proverbial last moment it was proved that it was all a frame-up and he in fact was the one being sexually harassed by the woman. He in fact was the good and faithful husband and father (though he had had a flowery past with the same woman), trying his best to safe-guard his marriage and family. He thanked them profusely for believing in him, trusting him and standing by him. One felt good. The actor was superb and convincing.

Living the Lie

But in real life, that very same actor is divorced, his children are obviously suffering from the same, and he has this other woman pregnant with his child. Reports in the papers show him the picture of health, his face radiant, his words to her, "What a difference you have made in my life."

But what about the lives of the wife and children. What happens to them. Is it merely a matter of settling them financially and in an amicable manner. What about their emotional and spiritual needs? Or is it that as long as one is married the motto that applies is: "We were made for each other" but when divorced, "Each one to his own....." ?

Moreover, what about the child conceived illegitimately? Few care to understand the psychological stigma, the hurt, the embarrassment and humiliation it goes through. Invariably, since such relationships are clandestine, the child ends up as a mistake, a by-product.

Other movies depict how the man is willing to go to hell and back, through humiliation and shame, through storms and suffering, all for the sake of saving his marriage. Why? It is obvious that the reason behind every movie is to impart a message. Regrettably, the ones imparting do not necessarily practice what they preach.

Still other movies depict the beauty of family. How, often enough husband and wife forgive each other and are united once again in trust. Still others, the necessity of treating children with respect and love, protecting them against the evils of separation and divorce.

Authors and script-writers have strongly advocated such themes and family values. The movies have taken them up, often using the best and most popular actors. Perhaps they have done so because the plots and story lines were unique and special. Perhaps, they were in it for the challenging roles and money to be made.

But more than likely they were also in it because someone believed in the message. A message that was/is needed for the time. Regrettably, while a super cast may put across the message most effectively to a wide audience, the message need not necessarily reach home to them, themselves. Why this great dichotomy or gap? Or is it all make belief, a scam, a joke?

Look at our beloved Rock Stars. The world's youth grow groggy over them. But ever so often their lyrics encourage illicit sex, divorce, violence and killing, drugs and the like. To their minds, acceptable music cannot be created any longer without such lyrics and themes. What the lyrics speak of, seem to fill an emptiness in the hearts and souls of their admirers. The very culture that is created, the life styles and values generated, are contrary to those that would keep families united and committed.

We can say that the pressures of life are too much to cope with. We can insist that the demands of the professions interfere with our relationships. We can even put a finger on the wars such as Vietnam and the Second World War. And this is all true. Yes there are factors that have devastated the psychology and spirituality of nations and peoples.

Families have been lost and broken up; family values have deteriorated and all but disappeared; there has been a clear shift of attention from family, others and community to the 'self'. Most of all God has been blamed for all the atrocities, aberrations and sufferings of life. But the ball does not rest there. Are we living up to our responsibilities by passing the buck and letting it lie where it falls?

Perhaps, if we had our eyes focused properly; if we had our heads on our shoulders; we might have made the necessary corrections along the way. We men continue to want to be in control; while women's lib fights to be freed of these 'chains', try to prove themselves equal to anything a man can do, put their careers first, before spouse and family. "I need to protect myself, my interests, my future. If you cannot fit in, if you cannot understand or adjust, you go your way, I shall go mine".

No, in general we seem to have gone along with the sweeping tide and undercurrents of our emotions and let them get the better of us. We allow our emotions and feelings to rule us. We allow the subjective therefore to be in control. In other words we permit the subconscious to take control and not the objectivity of our conscious intellectual minds.

Okay, one might feel that the spouse is no longer one's liability. But what about the children. As an adult, do you honestly believe that the children will not be affected by marital discord, by separation and messy divorce proceedings? Do you think "Well, I had to go through the same and I came out okay. If I could cope, why can't they? They will soon enough get over their traumas."

If this is one's attitude, I can only say you are playing games. You are playing games with lives, with tender hearts and minds. And you are responsible. If only you could understand and listen to those who come for counsel, to their tales of woe, their loneliness, their hopelessness.

People are longing to be loved. Their deepest plea, their incessant cry, their longing thirst and search is for love. And there is so little of that true love, going around.

The following is from an e-mail that has been doing its rounds. *"Are you aware that if we died tomorrow, the company that we are working for could easily replace us in a matter of days. But the family we left behind will feel the loss for the rest of their lives".* When a husband and wife separate and feel the need for divorce, the effect upon each other and upon the children is the same.

Isn't that what Mother Teresa called for, wherever she went and to whomever she spoke to —whether the common people or presidents and kings. Not that she had scant respect for the rich, the high and mighty. But she knew that in the final analysis; whether royalty or commoner, politician or voter, president or labourer, rich or poor; every one is human.

All are born naked and can take nothing with them, in death. No one is higher or mightier than the other. All are equal. Each one's needs are the same i.e. for acceptance, understanding and love.

No doubt we are living in an ever changing and fast world. But some things cannot. Dare not. The foundations on which humanity is based and depends upon, cannot afford to change i.e the family. However, the way in which we live family life, the way in which such basic truths are lived and expressed, may.

Example 3: Heather

I had forgiven my Mom at an earlier programme for being so very strict, expecting a lot of things from me, wanting me to be a perfectionist. But on the repeat I was shocked to know I had to forgive my Dad for being overloving towards me and pampering me, because of which I was expecting the same kind of attention from my husband. It was difficult for me to forgive Dad and let go of him, because I loved him so much, he made me feel so good and I did not want it to stop. I felt he did what I expected him to do for me. But I had to forgive him and be set free from expecting this kind of love, as I was finding it so difficult to adjust with my husband, expecting him to be like my Dad.

FUNDAMENTAL CONCEPTS OF:

MARRIAGE

The word 'Marriage' means the joining together of two single, independent units, thereby making them into one single whole. It means therefore the bringing together of two individual persons; man and woman, each with separate thought patterns, ideas, beliefs, ambitions, abilities and talents; to melt in the heat of love and sacrifice; in order to become one in thought, aim and objective. *It means losing your individual and separate identity as that specific man and woman.* The objective of this loosing and sacrifice is to produce a third unit called the home. A home of love, happiness and security.

We see this "marriage" commonly played out in the corporate world, bringing together large corporations, making them into one that is even larger. The two that were amalgamated have now lost their individual identities, but they bring together their separate strengths by way of people, products and services. These are pooled in, under new management, with streamlined

34

goals and targets. The main objective of such an exercise is to enable the New Company to reach further and further than the two were able to, in their individual capacities. To make this possible, certain cuts in staff, budgets and unimportant activities are undertaken to create and establish the identity of the New Company.

But unlike the corporate world, in this new marriage partnership, the wife comes first and is most important to the husband. First, before everything and anything else. More important than career, possessions and ambitions. In turn, what would she not do for him. If he is prepared to treat her as queen and *maharani,* would she not extend herself to the limit, for him?

Would she not be willing to put aside her own career and ambition in order to get such love, attention and security for herself. Would she not be willing to leave parents, home, personal ambitions and career, for the greater good of creating a home of love and security?

And so also, for the man, when his woman puts him first in her life.

Mashed Potato Salad. Love in marriage has to be like this. Before the mashed potato salad can be made, individual potatoes are chosen for their qualities and prepared by boiling. The final step in the recipe is to mash them and put them all together as one. They can be put together and made into one big ball of potato only when made soft and pliable on being boiled. Once together, there is no way of separating each from the whole. There is no way of identifying each potato from the whole salad. They have lost their individual characteristics and identity into the whole. The new identity, the new company, the new product, the marriage; is the salad.

COMMITMENT

Obviously to achieve such an objective, commitment to such a venture would be crucial. I can commit myself to teach the poor children, once a week. I can commit myself to a neighbourhood watch. I can make a commitment to visit you on a specific day and at a specific time. A commitment is a promise, an undertaking between two and more persons to achieve an objective, to attain a certain goal.

If any one party to that commitment does not keep his/her side of the bargain, that objective for which the commitment was made, can never be achieved. And there can be no doubt that in order to make a home as above, these two people must enter into a commitment, an agreement, a promise. Otherwise it can never happen.

Today in the corporate world, business transactions are often enough initiated and completed on the basis of trust. Deals are cut by word of mouth through the telephone. Data is sometimes accepted without necessary authentication. Such commitments in high-level financial arrangements find their way to completion. But unfortunately the same may not prevail with the Marriage of hearts and minds.

Marriage commitments can be/is the most difficult to live up to, perhaps because it takes determination and courage to prevail against all odds. The odds of rubbing against abrasive shoulders. The odds of having one's pride and prestige regularly and faithfully chiseled away. The pain and the glory of learning to accept your partner as he/she is. All this the partners are willing to do in order to build that home of love and security.

A marriage commitment for life can be the only basic value which, come rain or storm, cannot change. This commitment is a decision, a promise, a pact between the two parties to hand over each life to the other, saying, "my life is not my own any more, it belongs to you." The word commitment means to hand over, to surrender, to entrust to or to enter into (another's hands, control, influence).

People speak of "Temporary Commitments". They probably have mis-notions of the meaning of Marriage and Commitments. But marriage, unlike a business relationship or a job contract cannot contain clauses for its dissolution when the job is done.

Only a marriage partnership, calls for a complete and total giving of self to one another in every way – physical, emotional, mental, financial, social, sexual etc. unlike any other kind of partnership that might exist today, anywhere in the world. *For the simple reason that the job never gets done, until death.*

I have done it so far. And I have every confidence that I will succeed for many more years to come. Many, many others have done it, for twenty, thirty, fifty and more years of their lives. I have come across couples who have celebrated more than 60 years of marriage together.

Why cannot you. Are you less able and gifted, than they are. Is your Free Will and Choice being taken away from you. Are you weaker in the emotions, in your psychology. Are you less a man or a woman, than men and women used to be made?

At the time of making this commitment, the persons are aware that there will be problems to be faced, there will be differences of opinions and view points, there will be areas of disagreement. This is where the give and take comes in, this is where the dialogue and understanding comes in, this is where the forgiving and loving comes in.

Otherwise there is no point in such a commitment. You are willing to go through with all this, because of a commitment, a contract, a seal. Take away this commitment and you have marriage merely as a legality and a means to appease uneasy consciences.

Example 4:

While studying in England as a young man I met with a charming English girl and our friendship progressed into love. Though I asked her several times, to marry me, she never gave her consent except to say she did love me. She was the only child of an elderly widow who was against our marriage. I returned to India with her agreeing to follow me but we both knew it would never happen.

She married in England and I married a lovely talented girl. My marriage of more than 35 years has been very fulfilling with children and grandchildren. But often I would think about that English girl and wonder "What if ?".

Having attended the inner healing programme, through the inner healing therapy I forgave her and asked her forgiveness for hurt, pain, uneasiness, we caused one another. I was led to release her from my heart and hopes after so many years. I felt a great relief. The thought of her has never troubled me again.

LOVE

Along with commitment, comes love. What keeps that commitment lasting, is love. Not a love from feelings and emotions, but one that begins as a decision of the mind and grows to involve the feelings and the whole person. It is a decision to love that leads to the decision to commitment.

When a marriage is based on feelings, i.e., as long as both parties feel good and nice about the other, then there is nothing to sustain the relationship. Feelings/emotions come and go and can easily be influenced by stress, hurt and circumstances. When under strain, they are not strong enough to hold the relationship together.

Hurt emotions = I feel rejected = You do not love me.

If their loving is conditional, i.e., "I love you if you love me" then there is nothing exceptional about that. Why, even thieves can do the same with each other, as do criminals and rogues and back-scratchers.

Regrettably this is what the world is doing more regularly, taking their cue from those in the limelight, those who profess about it. Neither therefore is willing to give way.

Love however = Look here, neither of us is perfect. But we did find that something 'special' to bring us together in the first place. Let us get beyond our individual weaknesses, idiosyncrasies, hurts. Let us work it out.

Love means communicating, understanding, exercising patience, forgiving; not once, not twice, not only when it is easy or costs little; but on every single occasion.

GIVING

Love leads to commitment. Commitment does not only mean agreeing to be and do together. But how will that being and doing together actually materialize? This is accomplished by giving of the SELF to each other. Giving of all that is self. Giving of your whole being. This giving is expressed in many ways, the most intimate being through sexual union. Hence sexual union is a means of expressing love, expressing commitment to each other, expressing giving of each to the other.

The children produced are as a result of giving, loving and commitment. This giving, loving and commitment carries on now with each other and obviously with the children. The children are part of you. They have your blood and characteristics and nature. Your heart takes a leap each time you set eyes on them, each time they respond in their innocence and sweetness. You need them, to survive and grow in your inner being. So too do they need you.

Example 5: Howard

Two hours into the Inner Healing programme and I wanted to leave. You have to realize what such a programme meant for a business executive planning for marriage, an unspiritual person, a person caught up with the challenges of the world. But as I delved deeper I realized the importance of forgiveness and "clearing the air" as it were, for anyone who planned to begin a family. I would encourage all young people planning to get married to do this programme first.

Pre-Nuptial Agreements

This Marriage of two independent minds and hearts, this loosing of personal and separate identities, this mashed potato love, this giving of self; is based on a total and unconditional commitment to one another, is based on a trust like no other relationship or institution has known or could ever demand or imagine.

Therefore, pre-nuptial agreements have no meaning or place in such a marriage. Pre-nups pre-suppose mistrust of each other; a fear that one's assets will be eaten away by the other; an uncertainty about the lasting ability of the marriage. How in anybody's vastness of imagination can anyone enter into such an agreement and presume to live by the fundamental concepts of marriage, commitment, love and giving?

A pre-nup defeats the very purpose, idea, meaning and reason for marriage. A pre-nup can never constitute or support the idea of marriage in its true meaning and sense. Pre-naps are a deception and lay the base for a convenient alliance.

Breaking Up Is Hard To Do...

After years of living together, exposing and yielding themselves totally to the other; sharing the most intimate and exciting moments in their marriage bed, growing familiar with every tissue, muscle, mound and lump of fat, having the freedom to explore every nook and cranny of the other's body and sexuality; revealing the secrets and fears of mind, thought processes, feelings; bumping shoulders in the hallway, in the kitchen, in the toilet; entertaining guests and rearing children, the product of their intimacy, sharing, sacrificing and love; is it an easy matter for the couple to break up?

Contrary to the views and opinions that the media and especially the movies provide, breaking up is a hard business. It brings searing pain and wrenching of hearts and minds. Breaking up is not the only way out. There is no such thing as 'irreconcilable differences'. Yet, breaking up is an easy way out, a means to escapism; an escape from the truth, from sacrifice of self, from the hassles of commitment.

The media and modern philosophy would like to make out that there is no big deal in it. You have to do what you have to do. It might cause a little bit of pain and tears (similar to the bitch that has to give up its pups with a few sniffs and a whimper perhaps) but soon you will be able to find another companion. After all marriage is not a life long commitment.

40

But how many will testify to the intense pain, trauma and sleepless nights as a result of the break up. How many can share that their hearts have been torn, their confidence shaken and their trust broken. But because the need for companionship is so great each one will go through the process of procuring another friend, another relationship.

Yet again, half their lives are already over. Half their lives have been spent in producing and rearing children, by giving of themselves to spouse and children. How can they now presume to give themselves fully once again, in love and commitment, freely and without reserve; to someone new, who in turn has probably had a previous marriage as well.

Again, the movies seem to teach the ability and desire of separated parents to love their offspring, to visit and spend days with them. But the relationship with spouse is over. Do you not realize you are loving your spouse in that child, for that child is 50 per cent spouse. You cannot and will not cut off from the child, but you can from the spouse!

How can anyone love part of another and not the whole? Each time you set eyes on your child, you cannot but fail to recognize your ex-spouse's looks and mannerisms. Each time you hug that child with a send-off or a welcome-back, you are hugging and loving his/her father/mother, your spouse.

If you are one who allows yourself to be influenced by your TV, your movies and your novels, then you allow yourself to be led by the nose. Why do you not think for a moment? You, analyze it. You, apply this truth to yourself. Think for your children. Think for your family. Do what is right for them. Do what is best for them.

Imagine driving on the highway. You are doing a long journey from New York to San Francisco, to see your aged and ailing Father. As long as the foot is on the gas pedal you will move forward towards your destination. Should you say: I am tired, I do not feel like pressing down on the accelerator any more, the view is so boring; you gradually but surely will come to a grinding halt should you release the accelerator. You will not be able to accomplish what you set out to do. You will end up guilty and depressed at not completing your objective. Your father may never see you again.

The same goes for your marriage. It may not be an easy drive. There is no automatic gear transmission, controlled cruising or power steering. It is all manually operated; now cruising, now chugging uphill in first, now accelerating, now breaking. There may be trying times, tiring times, perhaps even so called wasted times. But keeping the objective in mind you will have the joy of knowing true happiness, true peace, true satisfaction.

Should it be at all possible to enter into another relationship freely, it cannot happen without first forgiving each other; without first getting rid of the resentment and anguish. Without first being healed of rancor as a result of being rejected, deposed, cheated and let down. Without first letting go totally of spouse and children. Without first becoming free again. Without first erasing all the loving, commitment and giving, that went into the making of that marriage as though it had never happened. Without first becoming *'Virgin'* again.

As if this were possible by some means known to God and man. Little do you realize that you cannot help bringing into the new relationship, your pain, anguish and animosity from the previous one. Perhaps even a certain amount of suspicion and lack of trust leading to an inherent insecurity. How long do we intend to fool ourselves. How long do we hope to play this game. How long do we want to put on masks that smile all the time?

Better to prick the bubble and descend to reality than live in bubbles of deception.

On the lighter side, what you can keep in front of you is the example of animals that are faithful to one partner all their lives. One such, is the bear! At a minimum perhaps, we could try to imitate them and give our spouse a bear hug each, every day.

The Big Question Therefore

Why cannot a family stay together. Why can't two people learn to communicate, forgive and remain committed. Why the need to separate and find other partners, to have other children. Why the need therefore to justify one's actions through arguments, rationalization, new philosophies and life styles. What therefore does one hope to achieve, derive and accomplish from Marriage? What therefore is man searching for?

Their decision to finally separate – is it based on *objective rationale* or *impetuous emotional pullings.* If marriage and all the perks that go with it does not seem to satisfy a man, is there something even deeper, at the base of each of the two individuals that has to be uncovered. Something that controls their decisions, relationships and life styles. Do we need to look into the core of man's inner self or can one say, hidden self, for the answer? If 50 per cent of marriages in the USA alone have been dissolved, what are we missing here?

Or was there some restlessness already prevalent within that man and woman, even before entering into the marriage? A restlessness, that does not permit man to stay together, committed, united and secure. A restlessness, that resists the giving up of individual identities, for the sake of a larger goal. A restlessness, that evokes anger, fear and guilt. A restlessness, that encourages selfishness and independence.

Finally, a restlessness that rebels against all authority and makes that man the only authority he needs to have. What is the nature of that restlessness? Where does it come from. What effect does it have upon man. This is what we hope to discover in subsequent chapters.

Chapter Four

HURT, THE SLIME
THAT MAKES THE WEB

*He entered Jericho and was going through the town
when a man whose name was Zacchaeus made his
appearance; he was one of the senior tax collectors and
a wealthy man. He was anxious to see what kind of man
Jesus was, but he was too short and could not see him
from the crowd; so he ran and climbed the sycamore tree
to catch a glimpse of Jesus who was to pass that way.
When Jesus reached the spot he looked up and spoke to
him: "Zacchaeus, come down. Hurry, because I must
stay at your house today". And he hurried down and
welcomed him joyfully. They all complained when they
saw what was happening. 'He has gone to stay at a
sinner's house" they said. But Zacchaeus stood his
ground and said to the Lord, "Look sir, I am going to
give half my property to the poor, and if I have cheated
anybody I will pay him back four times the amount."
And Jesus said to him, "Today salvation has come to this
house..."*
                                                    (Luke 19:1-10)

The above is an extract from the Bible. I have chosen it to
focus on the character of Zacchaeus. There is just one decent
sized para on him and yet the author found it important enough to
include it into the Bible. Let us find an explanation for it.

The Lie

Two points about Zacchaeus stick out strongly, one that he

was very short of stature and the second that he was a senior or chief tax collector. This made Zacchaeus, therefore, a very rich man. Now Zacchaeus was a Jew and in his capacity as a tax collector, served the Roman Empire. The Romans had conquered the land of the Jews and therefore were their greatest enemy. None other than God himself had promised this land to the Jewish people. Working for the Romans and to be identified as one of them, was the surest way of attracting the hatred and enmity of the Jews. Therefore, Zacchaeus a Jew, was hated by his own people, the Jews.

Now why should a man be willing to tolerate this rebuff and hatred from his own people? Why should a man who obviously had to be educated in order to serve the Romans in such a high post and knew fully well what that meant, be willing to face the rejection and hatred of his own people and community? Was it purely for the money?

As a young lad growing up in his village community and school, being very short in height, he would surely have experienced teasing, rebuke and being made fun of, by his fellow Jew boys. This form of teasing might be likened to what still takes place today, if not more crude and cruel. Name calling such as *'shorty'*, *'dade foot'* (in the Hindi language meaning one and a half feet), 'below sea level', or comments such as 'How is the weather down there?' would have been regular fare for him. He would have been singled out for fun and yet denied participation in their team games. All these forms of teasing and bullying would certainly have provided the boys a great laugh with much fun and enjoyment.

But, at whose expense, if not obviously, that of Zacchaeus? How was Zacchaeus, then a young lad, affected by all this. How would you have been affected and how would you have reacted, if it were your son or daughter who was the recipient of such treatment?

Without doubt Zacchaeus was a hurt child; hurt emotionally. He would have ended up in tears often enough, tears which he tried to suppress and hide from the others. Rage and anger, likened to a fuzzy drink shaken up till the gas is ready to burst

45

forth, would have been common experience to him, especially at not being able to hit back. And when he did try, the others who were bigger-made than he, would have roughed him up.

Rejection, unacceptance, fear, loneliness, anger and bitterness; would have been some of the emotions and experiences raging through his spirit, at different times and occasions. These experiences would remain with him the rest of his life unless someone could help him get over them.

Imagine young Zacchaeus growing up short and stunted, filled with a pent-up rage he could not express, describe or get rid off. On the one hand his hurt resulted in insecurity, lack of confidence, a poor self-worth or self-image. On the other hand there was this urgent need deep within, to prove himself; to · demand attention, to get people to recognize him and look upto him, to feel respected and important.

This frustration took the shape of an ambition he might never have normally developed. It lead him to the Roman Empire, the power that made all Jews in those days tremble and buckle down in fear, obedience and respect. They had no choice but to pay up and do whatever the Romans demanded. This was the way of getting back at his way and fellow-man. This was the way he would enact his revenge and punishment upon those who, many years earlier had hurt and abused him emotionally.

And this is exactly what he did. As chief tax collector, he had the power to tax at will or show clemency. He wielded his power to gain satisfaction, to placate the emptiness that lay at the depth of his heart. He enjoyed seeing his fellow Jews beg for mercy. He enjoyed having the power to grant that mercy or not. Perhaps he even enjoyed seeing the expressions of fear upon their faces. He would have taken full advantage of his position to force their respect, to force their acknowledgement and acceptance of him. It was not an authority and respect that he commanded, but one that he demanded, that he forced upon them from high. No wonder then, that they hated him.

The Truth

But Zacchaeus changed. What is it that brought about this change in him? What great miracle or thunderstorm had to take place before he could change his ways? Zacchaeus is mentioned in the Bible because he was in search of a man he had heard so much about. Jesus at that time was popularly recognized as a great prophet, a worker of miracles, a man who gave hope to the crushed Jewish spirits. To be recognized and respected by someone so greatly admired, made his day and changed his life.

When finally their eyes met, it was the acceptance coming from Jesus, respecting him as a person, that changed him. For the first time in his life he felt someone accept him the way he was; without condition, without question, without challenge or comparison. For the first time in his life he felt respected, important enough to be spoken to on a par, accepted as a human being and not for his power, his status or his wealth. For the first time in his life, he experienced love.

Like insects caught in a Web, no one escapes the Net...

Through this little story I believe the author is teaching that each and every one of us has a piece of Zacchaeus inside our hearts. All peoples of the universe be they rich or poor, educated or illiterate, having the support of social graces or not; every single human being that ever existed and still to come, throughout the globe, in every nation and race, of different hues and shades; like Zacchaeus is stunted and short of stature, not necessarily physically but most certainly in the emotions.

Every one of us is hurting from the traumas of life and relationships. Some experience outright rejection, unacceptance and a lack of love; others meet with fears, anxieties and worry; still others with domination and/or undue attachments of some kind or the other; and finally those who suffer from guilt feelings. The list is endless.

Example of Jaundice

Jaundice is one of the Hepatitis illnesses, which attack the liver. One suffering from jaundice suffers symptoms such as: yellowness in the urine and in the eyes, loss of appetite, paleness of the skin and such like. But these are only symptoms showing upon the outside of the body. These are indicators of what is truly happening within. The real illness is on the inside, i.e., in the liver.

Similarly this emotional hurt we are identifying are really wounds that take place upon the inner person, the inner spirit of the person. Wounds of rejection, fear, guilt and shame, inferiorities and such like. These hurts reveal themselves on the outside in various ways; through the body, through personality traits, through spiritual attitudes and aberrations.

The important point to understand and remember in all of this is: unless dealt with in some way either through counsel, psychology, some form of positive affirmation or prayer, these hurts will remain with us all through our lives and must effect our living, our values, our behaviour patterns and relationships. They can break up a home and ruin children; they can destroy marriages and families; they can pit communities against one another, set nations to war, prevent the making of peace due to feelings of threat and fear. Even preachers and priests, god men and gurus are subject to the net that inner hurt weaves around one, subtly and cunningly.

Marshall Tito is a well-known example. He was known for his persecution of the Christians in his country. This trait of behaviour has been traced to the hurt and humiliation that he received from the hands of priests when he was a little boy, serving daily Mass in his Church.

Napoleon is another example of a man short of stature, subjected to the cruelties of fellow students, a fearsome and demanding over-seer. A personality crushed and suppressed led to an ambition to rule the world, later to be dreaded and feared by the whole of Europe. This was his subconscious way of acquiring acceptance, respect, honour and recognition.

What about Hitler? Could his vicious domination of Europe and the world, be an offshoot of his childhood experiences at the hands of a tyrannical father, rejection by schools of art at which he had hoped to make a career, or the fact that his grand-mother was clandestinely impregnated by her Jewish employers?

In more recent times, we have seen the effect of hurt upon Presidents, Royalty and Politicians. No one escapes the net. For, we are only human and frail and imperfect. Love as we may, we receive and give hurt, sometimes aware but most often unwittingly and unintentionally.

Example 6: Bernadette

During the lunch break at a programme, we suddenly heard a loud wailing and anguished crying and realized it came from the hall where we had just concluded a session. It turned out that Bernadette had suddenly remembered the deepest pain in her heart that had taken place during school days. She was a bright student and deservedly should have received a prize for being the best all rounder. It was denied to her because her teacher had an anger and jealousy towards Bernadette's mother, who was also a teacher in the same school.

Bernadette was deeply distressed and felt the terrible injustice being directed towards her, due to no fault of her own. As she was unable to do anything about it, she was forced to suppress tears of pain, hurt and disappointment. Fourteen years later at this programme she was able to evacuate it through a process of forgiveness, thereby experiencing a deep peace. A short time later Bernadette was married and could claim that this was the best preparation she could have had for her new life, leaving scars and hurtful memories behind, never to trouble her or her relationship with her spouse.

Example 7: George

George was only fifteen when he came for one of our programmes. I was apprehensive that he was too young for such a programme and might not benefit at all. But he knew what we were about and put his heart and soul into it. He was petrified of his alcoholic and tyrannical father, who became easily violent under pressure. While going through the exercises (as detailed later in the book) to evacuate the hurt, fear and traumatic experiences he had received at the hand of his father; he became stiff with fear, fists clenched, chest heaving. This continued for some length of time until he was fully able to evacuate, let go and forgive. While doing the exercise, he was able to relive the traumas of home, now resolved and healed.

Example 8: Christine

Christine came to us sobbing that, fifth year into her marriage and she had not yet conceived a child. Her in-laws reminded her daily about her 'duty'. Her husband being under pressure himself would often take it out on her. When she attended the programme she got a deep insight into the effect of hurt upon her life and how it even prevented her from conceiving a child. Her story went like this:

Her own parents had expected a boy, longed for one and prayed for one, while she was growing in her mother's womb. Hence her deepest hurt was that of Rejection. She became quite a bit the man of the house, doing a lot of jobs that boys would normally do. She became a tomboy. Her menstrual cycle was most irregular with complications. It was only after a long time of waiting and a number of proposals that did not work out, that her parents managed to get her married.

Through the programme and after, she forgave deeply all those who had hurt her, consciously or unconsciously, such as her parents, her husband and in-laws. She embarked upon a journey of discovering and liking herself for who she was. Her subconscious gradually but surely got the message that she was a woman. The subconscious released its negative grip upon her bodily functions. One year after attending the programme we received the good news that she had become the mother of a delightful little baby.

The above are some examples of common experiences that people go through. Multiply them by a billion and you have the state of the general world. There will be variations of experiences, gradation of intensities, a range of ages at which they took place and the effect upon the person and his life. But all in all, each one of us has a bit of Zacchaeus in us, need to recognize that truth and deal with it through a process of evacuation and forgiveness.

This hurt is like a poison that eats into one, bringing a slow but sure death, robbing you of the charm of life, destroying all that is good. It is an acid that burns, a slime that stinks. It does not go away with a wish or merely because you command it to. Deciding to put the past behind you and begin life anew is not a full and complete solution. Time is no healer. Once inside, it lodges more and more firmly, reaping its harvest of brokenness internally and in relationships externally.

Example 9: Christopher

The point of this story is not Christopher's religious beliefs but how his experience in his mother's womb had far reaching consequences, implications, complications, running through and effecting the fabric of his whole life.

"Like every teenager just out of school I too had aspirations. I admired the stamina, zeal and strength of wrestlers. To live out my dream I did everything I could from joining a gym to sand bag practice. I was very passionate about it and decided to make it my profession.

After a few years of rigorous exercising and body-building I began experiencing excruciating back pain. I did not know what to do but I knew that I had to get better soon to get back into the game. Thus began my futile attempts at restoring my back.

All these efforts demanded a lot of time and large sums of money. I experimented with every possible form of medication and therapy: X-rays, physiotherapy, MRI scans, not forgetting the numerous trips to different

51

hospitals, e.g., Hinduja, K.E.M, Asha Parekh, Ramkrishna, Sion Government, Sanjivani, Cooper to name a few. In a span of five years and six months I underwent 3 MRI scans, was hospitalized for 13 days, was given 32 injections & tractions but to no relief.

I grew desperate and would act on any advice I received from people. So the experiments continued: yoga, sittings with masseurs, ayurvedic treatments, shark bone therapy, infra red belts, swimming, acupressure. It was really disheartening to see the time and money I spent on all these treatments and not one of them gave me even a little relief.

With all the pain, anxiety and desperation, my addiction to alcohol, cigarettes and substance (hash & grass) increased. I also made several attempts at ending my life, but something within me would not let me do it.

Finally when I lost all my strength to fight my illness and when I was on the verge of giving up, I was led to religion.

It was a beautiful experience. My life took a 180 degree turn. I wanted to give up all my old ways and live again. But the one thing I was not able to give up was my passion for Wrestling. Wrestling was a part of me, I could not imagine my life without it. I did not realize that I had made it my **god**. I could surrender anything else but not wrestling. And since I refused to give it up I was still bound .

Hence, despite making the retreat my problem persisted. In fact it worsened. I was confined to bed. I could not stand, sit or walk. All I could do was lie down. The doctors advised an immediate operation, with no guarantee of being healed completely. Failing which, there was every chance that I could be totally paralyzed, spending the rest of my life on a wheel chair. They diagnosed a Slip Disc. My spinal cord was twisted on the left side and had a long-standing swelling.

I had no clue what to do. Then I remembered I was clinging to my god of wrestling. As difficult as it was, I *finally let go. Since then I have been totally and permanently healed. My five years and six months of struggle ended on that beautiful day.*

I began helping other youth and though a preacher and councellor to them for 3 years, there was one thing I could not control. My anger. My anger could reach such pitches that it would lead to terrible violence.

For years I searched to be set free until I was able to identify the root cause of my Anger. This anger took its roots in my mother's womb. Mum used to be very angry with Dad for so many reasons. It was in this atmosphere that I was conceived."

For Christopher, his problems began in his mother's womb. His mother experienced hurt, injustice, rejection, anger yet with an inability to do anything about it. She had a need to express her views, a need to be loved and respected. Christopher picked up all these feelings deep in his unconscious. He became an angry and violent man. Wrestling became his way of proving himself to others. A time even came during his illness, when he could do nothing for himself.

He needed to forgive his mother and father, he needed to let go of his violence and anger, represented by his wrestling. He was able to do so through a religious belief and experience. To strengthen and deepen that belief and experience, he realized the need to consciously forgive through the Forgiveness Therapy.

Chapter Five

OUTER BODY AND INNER LIFE

Man is made up of a body, which provides *"Physical Life"*. A body that grows, generates, pulses, wears away and regenerates again, breathes, exercises, pumps blood and air, digests, walks and runs, perspires and relaxes. This human physical life begins at conception in the womb and progressively grows and takes shape.

Bodily organs such as the heart and lungs need some time to be fully formed to perform the actions and operations they are meant to. Traits and looks, shape and size, colour and complexion, attractiveness and beauty; are all fed in at the time of conception and are in due course of time realised, to be seen finally at birth and through life.

In the same way, qualities of emotions are also fed in, programmed and nurtured; which will be developed and realised in the person, through childhood and beyond. Personality traits and emotions such as joyfulness, friendliness, humour, fun loving, laughter, anger or fear, and so much more are traits that do not belong to the physical but to the *"Emotional Life"*.

What shape and characteristics that emerge, what specific behaviour patterns that surface, what negativities or positivities are stamped upon the individual, what identity is created; will only be discovered at a later stage.

Finally we have strength of character and determination, prayerfulness and attraction towards God, the Conscience and the ability to make Choices; all of which are traits at still a deeper level, that begin in the womb but bloom in later life. All this comprises the *"Spiritual Life"* which is uniquely different from the physical.

However, these aspects of the emotional and spiritual can be seen or expressed only through the physical body. When for example a little child giggles with glee, which is a physical action of the body, you know that the child is expressing emotions of happiness and excitement. On the other hand when the child is sad or frightened, you see the expressions of those emotions in its eyes or through tears. Anger can be recognised through physical gesticulating of arms and a strong and loud voice; cruelty can be seen in the physical action of beating the pet dog or tying up the bird, to its perch.

This speaks, therefore, of an inner life, an inner person, which exists very clearly but can express itself only through the actions of the body, the physical life. It is as though this inner life is hidden or masked by the body, ensconsed into the physical body.

Thus it is universally and intellectually accepted that man is not only physical body but a spiritual and emotional being, giving him an inner life, just as the body provides the outer life.

First Beginnings....

Now, we know that conception takes place when the sperm and the ova unite together. This logically explains only the physical life and its first beginnings. When and how does the inner life begin? Where does this inner life, this emotional and spiritual life come from? How does it germinate? What initiates it?

Some argue that the embryo becomes a full person, i.e., comprising an outer and inner life, only after the first few months in the womb. This seems to support their demand for abortion. Psychologists and case studies indicate that emotions are active from the very first moment of conception. Others say this life can enter only at the age of reason. This could range from anywhere upto the ages of seven or eight years of age. And yet little children are noteworthy for expressing emotions and feelings rather than intellectual truths. That is why they remain so cute and loveable!

Little children are also able to express a certain faith and trust in God. And this can only come from that inner life. I remember when I was a child, the story went around that the Communists, in trying to disprove the existence of God and the human soul, insisted that whenever they cut up a cadaver, they found nothing but physical organs and parts! How far this story is true, I do not know.

Is there any way of proving exactly at what stage this inner life, this life of the emotions and the spirit, unite together with the physical, to make a complete human being? Who can authoritatively dissect the physical from the emotional, from the spiritual? Who can again join them together at that precise moment in time to become one complete whole?

It is therefore an unspoken agreement and understanding that, this matter is left to the domain of religious beliefs and faith. Psychologists, theologians and others, among them the Christian Churches, believe that this emotional and spiritual life also mysteriously begins, all the way at conception. *A work of God.*

This inner life comprising emotional and spiritual is unique. It is distinct from the physical. It is a single unit which can be understood to be a soul or spirit or inner person. Without it, man is but a lifeless shell, a lifeless form, with nothing to speak of, with nothing of importance or worth. It is the spiritual and emotional qualities that give him identity, character and distinction.

The Three Circles of Life

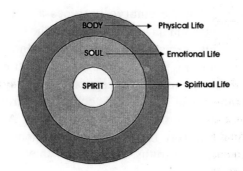

56

The Physical

Every human being can thus be said to have three major compartments, three facets, three aspects to life – the physical, the emotional and the spiritual. The outer most circle symbolises the body which provides physical life. It is this body that holds or contains the deeper and inner circles of the spiritual and the emotional. Man knows how to take care and pamper the body with clothes, food, accessories and perfumes.

When illness sets in, man knows that medicine, or a diet, or hospitalisation is required along with whatever treatment for the further well-being of the body. All seek this well-being or cure or healing of the body in order to live life smoothly. Without physical well-being, daily routines cannot be carried out without stress and strain to the body.

The Spiritual

The innermost circle symbolises the deepest core of the inner life, the innermost centre of one's being. We can categorise this as that part of the inner being wherein all goodness lies, wherein the deepest sentiments of one's heart lie, wherein one could say, God dwells. This is the area which provides spiritual life, a life that emanates from the spirit or soul that God has breathed into us.

This area of life could also fall sick. For those who believe, it would be called Sin. Sin and its definition refers to one's moral code of conduct and behaviour towards God and man. Breaking these moral codes or diverting from them for selfish reasons and motives, brings offence to others.

This results in disharmony within self and between self and God. Peace eludes us. Every human seeks "Peace", without which he cannot carry on life in an orderly manner. Healing of this area of life would also be required and could be obtained from a faith in God, by bathing in the holy river, by some work or act of penance, directly in prayer and meditation or through confession of one's sins.

The Emotional

Sandwiched in between, like a filling between two slices of bread is the emotional life. The life of feelings, experiences and reactions. Here lies our experiences with every relationship, at every word we hear, at every sight we see, at every thought we think and at every touch we feel.

Either we could feel positive or negative; accepted and loved, or rejected and unloved; secure, strong and confident or insecure, inferior and negative about oneself. We develop courage and freedom or are filled with fear and anxiety.

This then is the area of life we wish to deal with in this book. We can experience sickness in our emotions too, i.e. emotional hurt, wounds, scars. Hurts such as rejection, fears, guilt feelings, anger, misunderstandings and such like. But how do we begin to deal with this area. What can one do. Where do we go from here?

Firstly, we must acknowledge that for the vast majority, this is an area they have never been exposed to. They have had little reason or occasion to learn about hurting emotions. Life and all that she brings, is accepted as normal, from generation to generation.

Secondly, there are those who refuse to believe that the hurting emotions are of any great significance. Any shortfall can be overcome with a strong Mind.

Finally there are those who are of the opinion that everyone else but themselves need the doctor. Sadly, it is when one is too far gone with a nervous breakdown, that someone else has to take you to the psychiatrist.

Yet this is the aspect of life that needs the greatest attention, the greatest cure and healing, more perhaps than the physical or the spiritual. If we can believe and accept that the emotions have the greatest influence on the formation of the human character, then we must accept that the greatest time, attention and healing is required here.

Example 10: Greta

My father was alcoholic and used to abuse my mother physically. But I loved him dearly. My mother kept me away from him. Perhaps she did this to protect me but I had not realized that. Many a time she sent me away from the house and I felt rejected. Hence I never received love from my Mother and was deprived of my Father's love as well. Even when he was on his death-bed she prevented me from meeting him. I hurt and was filled with hatred towards her. I clung on to dad's soul for love and never let go of him.

I was molested by men, many times. Today I realize that in some way I was looking for a father's love even through the molestations.

I took to masturbation. I would steal money from Mum and only from her. I went against her in every possible way and said hurtful things to her every day for the past 7 years. I searched for love in my boyfriend. I had sex and never felt guilty. All my relationships started breaking all of a sudden because of my behaviour. I was irritated and stubborn and snappy. I was totally broken, confused, lost.

But as I began on my journey of forgiveness I felt free, healed, alive and happy. I had peace.

Uniqueness of the Emotions

Having identified the three major facets or compartments of every human life, one needs to realize that the three together comprise the human being. The physical, the emotional, the spiritual together make us what we are. Each can be identified separately and uniquely, but cannot be separated from the others. The three fit together like gloves and function like one. They cannot exist apart from one another. They cannot function independently. They work hand in hand, each supporting the other, each affecting the other, each building the other and at times even influencing the other in positive and negative ways.

Now just imagine this. Life begins at conception and there can be no argument about this. While a comparatively rapid process of development is initiated as the cells multiply and begin to take shape and form, the fullness of physical life however, i.e. the full body with organs and limbs and their functioning, will be seen only some nine months later.

In other words, while physical life has begun at conception, the proper functioning and physical activity of that life will begin only much later, such as movements and breathing. Even then full physical activity is not complete. The child now needs to learn to eat, swallow, walk and run and every other form of physical activity the body will demand and allow. This will take weeks, months and even years.

Hence for *practical* understanding and purposes, let us accept that there is almost no physical life and activity at the time of conception. Let this however not be construed as an argument for abortion. That is not the purpose and context in which this is written.

Similarly, spiritual and intellectual life is for all *practical* purposes non-existent at the time of conception though the making of a Mother Theresa or Einstein may already have been established.

Encouragement in the right direction over years of love and nurturing will result in the fulfilment of those seeds implanted at conception. There is no way in which growth can be measured. There is no way in which this spiritual life can be seen or witnessed or proved. Theoretically it can be claimed that a child conceived to very intelligent persons, will be an intelligent child. Or a child conceived to very religious and devout and loving persons, will have a greater bent towards the spiritual life. But this has to be seen much after conception and even birth.

However from the contribution that psychology has made over the years, it has been observed that emotional life, *practically speaking,* is fully alive and responsive, fully active and reactive from the very moment of conception in the mother's womb.

The emotions have no time frame within which they need to be prepared and developed before they can begin to work and influence the human person. They do not have to wait to be fully matured and ripened before their role in the development of the human person can begin. They are from the moment the sperm and ova meet, fully functioning, fully responsive. While they exist in full form, their training no doubt carries on in the womb and beyond depending upon the positive or negative strokes received.

The above can be expressed in terms of percentages, not to be statistically correct so much – as this may never be possible, as to get a better sense, a better grip and understanding of the subject matter at hand:

At the moment of conception:

Physical life – for all practical understanding   =   **1% active and alive**

Spiritual life – for all practical understanding   = **.01% active and alive**

Emotional life – for all practical understanding   = **100% alive and active**

The conclusions that can be drawn therefore is that the Emotions have the greatest role to play in the formation, the moulding, the shaping of the character and behaviour of the person. The size and health of the physical body too, can be influenced by these same emotions.

When you look at an adult, gauging his qualities for a job or responsibility, sizing him up for who he is and whether or not he can be trusted, assessing his character in order to give your daughter's hand in marriage to him; you do not look at outward appearances, at his physical qualities and abilities. You do not look only at his accomplishments and material successes.

You search for far more important qualities that speak of his personality, his true nature, his inner character. A character, that speaks of the inner life that is 'hidden' or 'covered' by the outer body. You look for goodness and integrity. Your eyes and ears are open to anything that might speak of suspicion and mistrust.

In fact this would apply to all persons. Who am I really? What kind of person am I? What are my strengths and weaknesses? The person that I show to the world, the real me, the real self; is not seen in the physical so much, as in the inner character that I convey somehow, through the outer body. The real me is inside – in my emotions, in my inner spirit.

Harry is a very timid person. Though his physical being is in good shape and comparable to Sylvester Stallone, his real self, the true Harry is scared of his boss and allows his wife to nag him.

Vanessa is a hot-tempered person, who yells and screams for the least thing, gets excited and animated by matters of least importance, though she is on the surface very petite in stature and delicate in looks.

Richard may be a preacher of God's Word and Wisdom to all around. The children flock after him. But in his heart-of-hearts only he knows how he trembles before God because of a spiritual weakness or sin.

Gillian had this compelling fear that, she would want to abort the child she might conceive. Through counsel it was revealed to her that the real child in her womb when there, was not just flesh and blood and bone and marrow. The real child in her womb was what was contained within that flesh and blood. The real child was the inner life, the life of emotions and spirit that was contained within the outer body of flesh and bone. She was able to overcome her fear.

In the good old days, persons with the highest IQ (Intelligent Quotient) would automatically top the list of contenders for job openings. People were rated purely by their Intelligence. In the 90's, the choice of candidate was also determined by his EQ (Emotional Quotient) - brilliance alone was not enough. The ability to handle himself and others, in any given situation was considered even more important. More recently, the SQ (Spiritual Quotient) is considered to be the most important criteria for appraising a person.

The SQ does not necessarily have anything to do with religiosity or spirituality. Religious beliefs being different, there is an inbuilt natural desire that each has been born with. The religion or spirituality one practices might emphasize and strengthen this inner quality. Religion can hone into and clarify or purify this inner quality, the spiritual intelligence.

SQ refers to the capacity not to be limited with logistics and reason, profit margins or measures of success. Not either, only in the ability to be suave and calm while dealing with difficult situations and especially when temperatures run high. Its true worth is in the ability to question those same motivations and targets with a:

"what is the final purpose of what we are doing?"

"How best can we make the people happy?"

"Why am I here?"

In other words it questions purposes, values, motivations. The understanding being that, the SQ is the fundamental and necessary foundation for both, the IQ and EQ.

How does the real inner you feel and think and behave? Who are you really? What are you really? Find out and you will have life.

An exercise – to become aware of the emotional hurts that an every day common-to-earth child might go through from the moment of conception in its mother's womb.

CONCEPTION

First of all, the atmosphere in which the child is conceived would begin the whole story. The circumstances of the parent's marriage, i.e., whether it was an arranged marriage or a love marriage (this would be important to clarify in eastern traditions), would influence the freedom, joy and happiness of sexual intimacy. Marrying against the wishes of the parents and the consequent lack of their support, lend tension to the early years of marriage. The absence of one or more of their parents at the wedding, can cause deep sadness, especially for the bride.

If the mother for any reason was forced to marry (as is common in eastern traditions) or was raped, the consequent conception certainly would not be in an atmosphere of peace and harmony. When a child is conceived outside that of wedlock or today through high tech scientific means; it would not be the consequence of a loving-giving between two persons. It would certainly miss out on that most crucial of ingredients – Love.

Trained in quaint and narrow understandings of sexuality, morality, behaviour and relationships with the opposite sex; can effect her openness to her spouse in the marital act. Giving of herself would be restricted and filled with fear and anxiety. Quite common in India is the need of healing for those married at very young and tender ages, sometimes as early as 13; while playing hop-scotch on one hand, having to give in to the demands of a husband at night on the other side.

For the first couple of weeks no one is even aware of the existence of this child. When they do become aware; they are not prepared, are afraid, feel guilty or even attempt to abort. Nine months in the mother's womb and the child is affected by all the mother goes through, such as, tension at home and at work, in-law problems, a demanding husband, alcoholic and drug-related tensions and traumas. Excessive physical work and financial difficulties can result in emotional tension for the child.

Example 11: Martha

When she first came for counsel, Martha was about 45 years of age. She would react apprehensively with fear, anytime she heard a loud or sudden noise such as squealing of brakes, excessive hooting of a horn, a factory siren. On analysis, this was traced back to the time she was in her mother's womb, during the Second World War. Her mother would react in fear (like most people would) to air raid warnings and sirens. Making her aware of this root cause, taking her through counsel and prayer cured her of these irrational fears and reactions.

Example 12 : Janet

During a general session of counsel and prayer for healing of past memories, Janet was found to be wriggling and squirming on the floor, crying with the pitch, tone and expression of a new-born baby. On questioning her later, it was found that her mother had laboured long and hard in giving birth to her. That had left emotional scars of trauma, pain and fear, which remained with Janet all these 37 years of her life. During the prayer session, she found herself actually going through a process of being born again, of emerging through the birth canal, but this time rid and healed of the traumas that lay with her all this time. The baby's loud crying was a process of releasing the hurt after all these years.

BIRTH

The birthing process can be traumatic to the child especially if mother has complications such as: being a breach case or necessitating the use of forceps or being born by caesarean section. Fear at delivery of the first child and lack of husband's presence at birth, leads to anxieties. Every emotion the mother goes through is passed on to the child. Little embryos, infants and children at the breast do not analyse, think out the hurt and work it out in their minds. They only feel. They either feel accepted, loved and wanted, or rejected, unwanted and lonely.

On being born, some of the early reactions from parents, Grandparents and others could resemble this: "Yuck, the ugliest ever." "Mum how could you do this to us? What will the neighbours say?" "He is just too dark (or white or mixed), he has absolutely no hair and his nose is too long."

Example 13: Clara

Clara was a hard woman in all her personal and business dealings and relationships. While she did feel for people, she always gave the air that she did not. She seemed to be cold and insensitive to the needs of others. Tracing her background, she was the first among many children, of parents who ran away from home to be married. Her mother came from a wealthy aristocratic family, her father a 'commoner', not highly educated or financially strong. The families were against their marriage so they eloped and married against their parent's wish.

They had to struggle very had the first few years. Her mother who was used to servants at her beck and call for any and every need, now had to work and slog as though she was the servant of the house. She was used to a rambling house with plenty of garden space to run around in; now she had to content herself with a tiny apartment with little air to breathe. Knowing her parents were unhappy at her choice of husband and especially for eloping, she could not ask them for help be it financial or otherwise at her time of need. And at her first delivery it was not with excitement and joy, but trepidation, that she informed her parents.

It was under this strain, this tension, and this lack of freedom that Clara was conceived and born. The negativity she was exposed to had its effect upon her and shaped her character for life. Counsel and prayer helped her no end to relax with herself, to accept that she was acceptable, to accept her background i.e. parents who came from a different cultural, financial and social status.

Example 14: Eric

Eric was an angry young man who could not control his sexual involvements with the young ladies. His mother was married off against her will to an old drunkard because her parents were anxious they might not live long enough to settle her. She used to be a vivacious, vibrant young lady, popular in a healthy way with all the young men in the town, an expert pianist and musician.

All that changed overnight when she married. She never

was able to love her husband, had a tough time with him and grew old and grey much before her time. Obviously, having been forced to marry a man many years her senior, she never was able to give her heart, soul and body to him freely and in love.

Eric and his siblings were conceived in an attitude of resignation, anger and unforgiveness (towards her parents). Eric never really experienced his mother's love and all his life was searching for the same, unknowingly, through his many sexual exploits. He had to learn to forgive his parents and his grand parents for making it all happen.

THE FIRST FEW YEARS

Comparisons are one of the most destructive emotional strokes children can ever receive. Belittling, ridicule, abusive language and harsh words; physical violence and abuse; domination and strictness which leave scars of fear; over attachment, possessiveness and high expectations; all lead to inflicting insecurity, inferiority and a poor self-image upon the child. The child grows up to feel incapable of doing well. The child will believe this is the truth about itself and all its life will be affected accordingly.

Being teased and called nick names, feeling left out by others, the very first day of school, fear of an alcoholic father, being witness to violence and quarrels between parents; all these negative inputs have the power to destroy a child, to inflict life-threatening attitudes and beliefs in himself; to become in turn violent, dominating, alcoholic. In turn the same traits are passed on to one's offspring.

CHILD BATTERING AND SEXUAL WOUNDS

Common enough among children of both sexes, leaves scars for life. Violence begets violence. Being a victim of regular sexual abuse makes one inflict the same upon others. Such traumas leave their mark and grip upon the child, through the subconscious, influencing it and determining its behaviour when an adult.

Violence, sexual abuse, paedophilia, sexual perversions and homosexuality are signs of the inner person attempting to satiate the inner needs, attempting to fill the emptiness in one's heart, attempting to find the love which has been missing.

THE FOUNDATION STONES

True acceptance, love and nurture from a mother and father are the basic foundations and pillars for the emotional growth of every human child. No one, no matter how kind, holy and good, can replace the love of parents. Death of a parent, separation due to divorce or work situations, being left with baby sitters or at crèches, the inability to express love for the child; causes the child to feel "Mum and Dad do not love me".

A bridge collapses invariably because its foundations are weak or have weakened due to shifts and changes in the soil or currents. A building collapses due to placing too much weight upon its foundations which were never meant to take on such a load. People need to visit shrinks and even end up with nervous breakdowns because there was a crack, a weakness in the foundations that were laid; when conceived, born and brought up as children.

On many an occasion relationship problems, marriage difficulties, the so-called generation gap with children have been traced back to, lack of suckling at mother's breast. Lack of parents love leaves the child bereft of the greatest security, strength and confidence it could ever need. Especially in this day and age of test-tube babies, artificial insemination, surrogate mothers and resulting court cases and disputes, it is always the child who suffers; who suffers the most.

Example 15: Frazer

Frazer is a dentist and has a family. But for many months he suffered fear, confusion and insecurity. His greatest fear was that he might by error cause pain and suffering to his patients. This fear took such a hold upon him that he was unable to attend his clinic for months.

*Having analysed his case, the following pertinent points came
to light:*

1. *His parents married against their parents wishes.
   Between the two of them there was a substantial
   difference in their financial, cultural and social status.
   They were married in another country without either of
   their parents being present. In an Indian tradition, the
   presence of family is most important at such an occasion.*

2. *Consequently Frazer's parents struggled for many
   years, especially financially.*

3. *Frazer was conceived immediately and born only nine
   months after marriage. His parents were definitely not
   prepared for a child so soon. They were still struggling
   to get settled in, and to find their way.*

4. *By the time Frazer was three, his first baby sister was
   already born. One day mother asked him to check in on
   baby and see if everything was alright. He did so. He
   noticed baby on her stomach, face into the pillow,
   sleeping soundly. He reported that all was well.
   Fortunately, something put his mother on alert. She
   double-checked, only to find baby already turning blue
   in the face due to asphyxiation. Frazer was reprimanded
   seriously.*

5. *At the age of six and a half, Frazer was placed in a
   boarding school. He remembered how much he missed
   his parents. He cried many a time into his pillow.
   Whenever he had to part company with them, after the
   holidays or after a visit from them, he would beg and
   plead with them not to leave him. He remembered how
   he would return to school with a sinking heart, tears in
   his eyes, his spirit full of apprehension and fear.*

Conclusions drawn:

1. Frazer experienced at his deepest root level - feelings of
   rejection, since his parents were not ready for him when

he was conceived and brought into the world. Their background tension and struggles added further to the rejection. Putting him into boarding school (while a necessity due to circumstances) almost perfected the feelings of rejection as Frazer continued to miss his parents attention and love.

2. Missing out on parental acceptance, love and attention, resulted in deep insecurity and a lack of confidence in himself and his working ability. This lack of confidence grew steadily as he missed the love of his parents more and more.

3. Added to this basic weakness in his psychology comes the incident where his baby sister almost dies due to what he came to believe was negligence on his part. This experience added to the rejection and lack of confidence he felt, when reprimanded.

4. Any request to help with his sister or do house chores, would remind him of his near fatal mistake, adding to his rejection and lack of confidence.

5. The two root hurts joined together to make him a perfectionist, not out of wanting to be precise and exact, but out of a need to be accepted and appreciated. If he performed well, in fact perfectly, there would be no fear of hurting anyone, there would be no reason to give cause for rejection. This was a pressure that weighed upon him.

6. His acceptance, his appreciation, his self-image, depended directly upon his performance and success. Not upon the person he was/is, not upon the person he was created and meant to be.

7. This spoke of an in built fear that charged him, manipulated him, controlled him. One fine day it happened. Due to a minor error on his part, someone did experience pain in the dental chair. This incident acted as the trigger for what was lying deep within. Ever since then the fear, the insecurity, the lack of confidence, the rejection, reared up like a guard dog on its hind legs ready

to bite off the intruders head. He went through immense turmoil, confusion, and depression. As a result he has not been able to attend the clinic.

Example 16: Noel

It was some time in 2003 when I reached a stage in life when I was confused and felt life was meaningless. I attended the Inner Healing programme hoping to find peace and understand myself better. Through the counselling session a very clear picture of my childhood emerged. When I was in kindergarten, I had to spend the mornings in a creche. This was because my parents worked the whole day and I had afternoon school. I hated that environment and could not understand why my parents sent me there. I remember my dad dropping me off there every morning and I hated him for it. I felt rejected.

He would also occasionally beat me and my brother. I remember on one occasion I returned home alone from school by auto-rickshaw instead of waiting for my dad to pick me up. When he finally came home he gave me a thrashing. I couldn't for the life of me understand what went wrong. I certainly didn't mean to waste money. This is one of many examples that indicate his temperament.

Today, I can justify everything he had done. And I know whatever he did was for my own good. However those acts still lead to me hating him. Those days transformed me from somebody calm to somebody stubborn, impatient and short-tempered. I looked at my father as someone cruel, violent and uncaring when in fact it was the opposite.

Before the programme, these were nearly forgotten memories silently eating away at my subconscious. I would rebel against my father for no apparent reason. I would blame my parents for my failures. But gradually, as I continued to forgive and the process was complete I began loving him. Things are excellent today and getting better.

To add the icing on the cake, while serving at a youth camp I was able to help another young man who had a similar problem with his dad, only much worse. He had a stammering problem and I guessed it was because of the fear his dad put into him. I explained to him this forgiveness therapy and made him do it. By the end of the camp, his stammering had disappeared!

In the case of Noel, he was successful in all he went about. His career was on the rise as a sea man. But slap in the middle of it, he was troubled as above. The roots being not in some recent developments on board ship or with his seniors but with his childhood as explained.

Love: The Eternal Foundation

The discoveries of the sciences indicate that the Emotions are the most influencing factor in the formation of the human person. They form the foundations upon which the nature and quality of that person develops.

Foundations provide a base, a strong platform upon which further construction and development can take place. This further development and construction can take place depending upon the strength of the base. Engineers therefore while calculating the total weight that has to be built, such as a bridge or a building, then design the foundations and pillars on which that whole weight stands.

A foundation of love provides the energy and motivation for the entire spectrum of a person's life. His physical health, his spiritual freedom and his emotional well-being are all directly dependent upon those foundations. His youth, his accomplishments, his sexual encounters and escapades, his marriage and his parenthood, his meaning to life and the future, his relationships at home and around, all can be healthily built upon and around a foundation of love. This foundation provides strength of character, integrity and wholeness to life.

This therefore provides the answer to **The Big Question,** at the end of chapter 3. More often than not, individuals enter into marriage, already traumatized by their childhood. Their foundations are weak, unstable and falling apart, having seriously missed out on love in one way or the other. Hence the building they attempt to construct, i.e., the marriage and home, can never stand firm and permanent.

Missing out on love as children, they are left feeling unaccepted, unwanted, empty and insecure. They now enter into marriage bringing with them this unwanted and undesirable baggage. They begin this new life, not as two wholes but as two incomplete persons. They believe marriage will solve all their problems. They believe, whatever they have missed out on in their individual lives, can be replaced through marriage and family.

But in this institution of Marriage, demands are made of them of the following kind:

1. Acceptance and love of spouse as he or she is.
2. The call to lose ones identity for the larger whole
3. The sacrifice and giving of self for the larger good, i.e., the family.

= GIVING

But all of this giving, costs too much. Each in themselves is not complete and a whole. As persons who are not complete and whole in themselves, they are unable to generate the love needed, persistently and without fail, to build their home. The bank deposits of filial love are not solid enough to attract interest, in order to keep going. What they do not have, what they have not received, they cannot give. Rather, they find themselves eroding whatever little reserves they possess and soon reach exhaustion.

Losing their identity for the sake of the larger good, the family; becomes an impossibility. Rather than giving and sacrificing, they find themselves struggling for survival. The survival of an identity that already feels threatened in its 'incompleteness'. In order to survive, they begin to look inwards to themselves.

This struggle thus leads them to become performance-and-achievement-oriented. They are more concerned about safeguarding interests, careers and identities. They hope to gain the recognition they have missed out in their early childhood, through these achievements. They become independent, adamant about their ways and desires, putting their needs and plans before that of family. When this takes place, the very basis on which Marriage is founded, is cut from under their feet and the house (instead of home) that Jack built, is bound to come crumbling down.

This then is the restlessness that exists in many a heart, even before it can join up with another in matrimony. This then is the emptiness of the inner spirit, the inner man, that yearns and longs for recognition, appreciation and acknowledgment. This then accounts for the weakness and cracks in the foundation, the base, upon which two people might hope to build their home. This therefore is the cause of so many broken and failed marriages.

Many marriages have been saved from total collapse, when the parties have humbly taken the advice given and worked upon their childhood hurts. On many an occasion, young couples have been cautioned to deal with their childhood traumas before tying the final knot, lest they destroy one another.

Extracts of Testimonies:

....*I was depressed for a long period of time and was unable to smile. I realized I had indulged in occult practices and New Age philosophies, which had taken control of my mind and eaten me from within. It also came to my realization, the hurts lying in my subconscious and unconscious.*

My life had been one long search for a father's love. Daddy had been away on work from my early days for 20 long years, as a result I missed him sorely and longed for him.

....*I had been diagnosed with a cyst on my left ovary and was due for an operation. Attending various spiritual programmes the abnormal bleeding slowly reduced and almost totally passed away. However I was encouraged to attend the Inner Healing Programme as severe pain continued. I realized that I had missed out on parental love as a child, especially the fact that they wanted a boy when I was born. While in prayer I felt something poking me in the uterus. Two days later there was a vague thought that I was missing something, something was not quite normal; till I realized that I had been set free from the excruciating pain that had troubled me.*

....I was a sensitive child, quick to anger with other unhealthy emotions, which in turn brought about illness such as allergies, breathlessness, headaches caused by sinusitis.

.... I tried all kinds of medication such as allopathic, homeopathic, ayurvedic, yoga, meditation, the works. I still continue with my sprays and tablets. Till it was pointed out to me that it was in the womb that I experienced rejection from my mother

...Doing the Therapy left me in pain, discomfort and a heavy head. I kept forgiving all I could remember who had hurt me till I remembered what I was told about my delivery. Mum was very serious. Doctors could not guarantee that Mum and the baby to come would survive. They made Dad sign a document choosing either her or me. He chose mum. As it happened we both survived. This was the greatest and deepest wound I had to be healed of.

Chapter Six

AN ATOMIC EXPLOSION

Having had a glimpse into the beginnings of hurt and their effects upon the child, it is time now to understand the more serious implications of these hurts throughout every area of life. For our base of operations we shall once again refer to the diagram in the previous chapter, depicting the three main circles of the human life as physical, emotional, spiritual.

1. How Hurts Affect The Emotional Life

Introduced now to emotional hurts and the different ways in which they can enter, what affect do these hurts have upon the emotional characteristics, behavior patterns and personalities? Some may experience rejection and loneliness; others anger or fear; others inferiority and insecurity; and still others timidity or the need to be dominating and having one's own way. This is only a beginning.

A million people will have a million different characteristics. Given any set of circumstances such as an alcoholic father, no two persons in the same home will be affected in the same way. One might become a timid, fearful clerk/assistance in an office, the other a hot-tempered, ambitious executive.

A child might be hyperactive, troublesome, sickly. A teenager gets addicted to drugs and alcohol. A married person becomes unfaithful to the one he/she pledged his/her love and loyalty to. A bank manager finds the need to scream at his subordinates. A couple married for twenty years feel empty, hollow and dry.

Example 17 : Margaret

Margaret is a school teacher who married the man she fell in love with. She has three children all of whom have not met with her expectations. Their complaint is that she is too possessive and interfering. Her husband complained that she was suspicious of him and hurt his feelings deeply. Her letters to him only contained complaints about his "so-called" unfaithful relationships with other women. She lost her teaching job due to her suspicious nature.

We met her husband who was very much a family man of good character; patient, forgiving and hardworking. What could be wrong? What made Margaret behave as she did? Where lay her crying need for love?

The answer we found soon enough. Her parents had an earlier child whom they had named Margaret and whom they loved very much. Regrettably at the age of eleven she died due to an incurable illness. This broke their hearts as Margaret was the center of their lives. As soon as another daughter was born they named her Margaret (i.e. the Margaret we knew and were dealing with) and loved her with all their strength.

Unfortunately and without realizing it, her parents were really loving Margaret the first and not Margaret the second. Margaret the second was only a reminder to them, of Margaret the first. And hence though they had showered upon her their love, Margaret the second did not experience any of their love in her heart. She could sense deep in her inner-being that whom they were really loving was her elder sister who had died. She felt used as a rag doll and rejected.

But this hurt was not experienced at all in her conscious mind but in her subconscious and even unconscious. In other words she was not at all aware of what was truly hurting her and controlling her life.

Her whole life you could say was ruined by this experience. She developed feelings of rejection, mistrust and suspicion. Her relationship with her husband and children, her motivations and understandings, her idea of life and its meanings; were all influenced negatively and tainted permanently. As a result she caused pain to herself and the ones who loved her the most; her nearest and dearest. The saddest truth being that, her finger pointed at everyone else except herself; there being no truth in her suspicions and accusations.

And so we see how hurts affect our basic attitudes towards self and others; played out in inferiorities and superiorities, hatreds and guilt feelings, insecurities and fears, pride and arrogance, timidity and apprehensions.

The 9 months in the womb and the first 7-8 years of our life, are understood to be the formative years. All the input, whether positive or negative, begin to form our attitudes, shape our behaviour and mould our character. Our thought patterns, our speech, our actions are all a result of this shaping and moulding.

Other basic emotional patterns may take the form as under:

Feeling insecure. Lacking Confidence. Having a poor self-image and even hating one's self. Fear of people, inability to speak into a mike, etc. This will be dealt more in detail in Chapter 10 – Getting to the Heart of Things.

Often times people in frustration might say " I have tried so hard to change. I have to reconcile to the fact that this is the way I am." And probably they have tried everything to become a more loving person, a less angry person, a more trusting one. The question that could arise is:

Are we born negative in nature or have we been shaped and formed thus. e.g. A person filled with fear and anxiety. Could that be the natural characteristic that person has inherited from his/her parents at conception, or was fear and anxiety programmed into that person during the formative years, possibly beginning at conception within his mother's womb. The latter is what most schools of psychology believe. Therefore the statement "There is nothing I can do about it" is a misnomer.

2. How Hurts Affect The Physical Life

We have spent some time in the previous chapter and above getting to know the emotional hurts and their effects upon the inner person, the inner man. How can these hurts which are seen in the middle circle of the diagram now extend their influence and affect the physical life. In other words how do these hurts cause physical sickness and illnesses, reaching out now to the outer life, the body?

Example 18 : Bernadette

"On the first day of the programme we were told to keep a note of our dreams. This is the dream I had:

I was cleaning my neighbours house, keeping all the dirty rags for washing. I realized this was the beginning of the cleansing of my heart. Then I saw myself walking along with my two small daughters down the road where my mother lived. Suddenly the climate changed. A strong wind blew and there was a sign of rain. I have a phobia towards water. I realized that my daughters would get wet and I would have difficulty in wading through the muddy waters. When suddenly a small boy carrying two umbrellas approaches me. I awoke with a start.

My counselor explained there was unforgiveness in my heart. I could not understand what he meant and whom I had not yet forgiven though I had just made a most sincere confession of my sins.

During the afternoon siesta my room-mate asked me about my brother's death. I narrated to her the whole incident, that due to a family feud someone had strangled him to death. While I was narrating this, it suddenly struck me that it was my younger brother's death that had affected me the most. He was six years old. I was ten. I had never forgiven those persons who were involved with my brother's death. A guilty conscience always kept pricking my mind that he would not have died if only I had taken him along with me to play, when he asked me. While I was out at play and he was alone at home, those neighbours took the opportunity and strangled him, placing him in the water tank to make it look like a drowning accident. All my life I believed that I was responsible for my brother's death, that I had murdered my brother.

For fifteen years I had been plagued with Arthritis. Every specialist available, I had seen. Each one demanded a new battery of tests. Much money had been spent on my illness, to no avail.

As I did the forgiveness therapy, asking forgiveness of my brother for the guilt in my heart and forgiving those involved in his murder, I wept bitterly like a child. It was the washing of my heart. I felt light. After this I was healed of my arthritis and today I am without medicines for my arthritis."

To explain the background. Bernadette's parents had gone out for the evening, cautioning her not to go out to play with her friends, lest her little brother join her and get hurt outside. Unable to control the temptation to play outside, when her friend invited her, she proceeded to join her, leaving the front door opened. Caught up with her play, she had not noticed time going by.

It was dusk when her parents having returned called her inside and asked her to bring her little brother as well. Then began the long and eventful search for him. The police were called upon the scene and he was finally found drowned in the well. In their pain and sorrow they would reprimand her every now and then, reminding her of her disobedience, which had cost her brother's life. She grew up with guilt feelings, that she had murdered her brother. If only....

Unending testimonies can be shared of physical healing taking place after inner hurts have been dealt with. Healing of aches and pains, migraines, heart problems, pussing boils and diabetic wounds. This is the testimony of Augustine who was given three months to live.

Example 19 : Augustine

At a conference, I met up with an old friend, Augustine, after many years. I was about to thump him on the back out of the sheer joy of seeing him when he remarked "Hold it, if you want me to land up in hospital then go ahead". Rather surprised and taken aback, this is the story as narrated by him.

"Seven months ago [i.e. in May 1993], doctors in Bombay's Hinduja Hospital diagnosed me as suffering from homocystenuria, a metabolic disorder. This explained the severe bone pains that I had been complaining of for nearly two years and my medical history of complaints of pain and discomfort in my back extending as far back as 22 years ago. Those who knew me well knew that to touch any bony part of my body with anything more than a mild tap, brought excruciating pain; and occasions of severe contact even left me unconscious with pain. The disease is rare, discovered rather recently (1962), and as at the present level of research having no known cure. Medication to alleviate my pains proved of no avail."

Bombay's (now Mumbai) Hinduja Hospital is reputed to be one of the finest in the city and the country, with a highly trained and reputed medical faculty. Augustine was given three months to live given the progress of the disease. They accorded him free medical checks and tests as they were delighted to have such a rare illness in their midst which they could study at such close quarters. At the conference where we met, he moved around with fear and trepidation. Swatting mosquitoes on any part of his body, left him in agony.

"Literally thousands prayed for me that I might receive a healing; but I continued to deteriorate and suffer in pain. Until May 1993. Thanks to this avalanche of prayers, more proximately a visit to the shrine of Our Lady of Mount Carmel on May 9, and specific prayers for inner-healing, forgiveness and the releasing of bonds that bind, I

81

experienced a healing - a complete freedom of all bone pains in my body - despite being soundly and solidly stroked on my back!

Am I medically cured of homocystenuria? I do not really know. What I do know is that having beseeched the doctors to relieve me of my pains they could not do so."

During those days of the conference, i.e., May 10 –12, 1993, another old friend of his, totally ignorant of all Augustine had gone through, actually did thump him on his back having met him after a gap of many years. That is when Augustine realized he was healed of his pains. That was more than 12 years ago. And he was supposed to live for only another three months.

As you can see, Augustine was a man of faith and trusted very much in the power of prayer. However, what seemed to specifically bring a healing to him was the process of 'inner-healing', i.e. healing the hurts and traumas in his life, such as rejections, jealousies, suppressed anger and such like. These hurts had the effect upon him of being 'sucked upon', bringing to him a gradual but sure death. It was as though his very life was being sucked away.

These experiences in the emotions over the years, was transferred to the body. The body became an exit point for these emotional traumas and pressures. Therefore the pain experienced was an outward sign of his life being sucked away unto sure death. Having made him go through a detailed forgiveness, acceptance and love of self, in and through counsel and prayer, he was able to share his experience as above. Augustine's case is documented at the hospital.

Example 20 : Erika

Finally I share the case of Erika, thought to be suffering from CFS, Chronic Fatigue Syndrome. When we encountered her, we knew nothing of this illness but came to understand that CFS was far more widespread and of a great concern in America. Medical Science had not yet been able to study CFS in detail for the simple reason that it was still pre-occupied with AIDS. Much later her illness was finally confirmed to be Extreme Sleep Apnea or ESA. This is the story of Erika :

She was constantly tired and fatigued. Every morning she would wake up feeling exhausted. Having barely done a few jobs in the house, she would need to rest. She had to force herself to do simple house chores and by the afternoon had to drag herself to bed, sometimes on all fours. My heart went out to her because I could see she was a very lovely person, had a lovely family and home.

Medical Science has this habit of diagnosing an illness and no matter how rare it might be, providing it with a name. Providing it with a name gives it an identity. It is unimportant or of no consequence, how that illness got there. Yet, this is of key importance in treating it. In my experience, extreme and unnatural physical fatigue is due to a kind of mental struggle, something one is trying to get to grips with. Something one is battling with. Hence, my first question to her was, "what are you struggling with?" Out came the answer, mixed with sobs and tears.

Unknown to herself, she was expecting again. Wondering why she was spotting / bleeding, the doctor suggested a DNC without checking for pregnancy. Later, she realised that she was actually in fact carrying a child in her womb, which now would be deformed and hurt due to the DNC. Doctor advised a total abortion. She could not get herself to accept such a plan of action because it was totally against her belief. It was confirmed again that the child would be deformed, was advised abortion and under great stress gave in.

What she could not get to grips with, what she could not understand is how she, who was a Right to Lifer all the way, trying to live her Christian faith and beliefs in the most meaningful way possible, could ever have been party to an abortion or action that lead to the death of a child in her womb. She could not forgive herself for it. She had not yet come to terms with it. Such a simple thing as being pregnant, how is it that it had escaped her? This is the horrible struggle she was going through night and day, now two years later deep in her subconscious.

Mental struggles; struggling with ideas and decisions; trying to understand and work things out in the mind and not getting anywhere close to an answer or solution; can often enough be even more tiring and exhausting than physical labour and hard work.

Are all Chronic Fatigue Syndrome or Extreme Sleep Apnea patients going through the same mental and emotional struggle? Probably. While abortions can be had a dime a dozen, and women seemingly undergo the same without blinking an eye; there still remains deep down in the conscience, an awareness and knowledge that all is not as well as it is portrayed to be. Guilt, hatred and unforgiveness of self, remains. And of course there could be other reasons and occasions and struggles within the human mind that brings on fatigue.

Example 21: Preema

As I sat in a corner for the sessions, I felt conscious that all eyes were on me due to my severe psoriasis. During the sessions my discomfort increased as I began feeling wet waist down, squirming in my seat. When I checked later, my legs were bad, had cracked, were oozing, my clothes were stinking, my feet were swollen and horrible-looking. I thought I might have to return home. That night I kept tossing and turning as the room smelled increasingly.

But I was determined to be freed from this plague and during the counseling session was told that it was all to do with 'sexuality'. I thought skeptically this is another Freudian nonsense. But I was troubled by this thought and approached another counselor. The hurt of my brother sexually abusing me resurfaced and reliving the experience during the Forgiveness Therapy was traumatic. I sobbed like a baby.

I also realized why he had harassed me all my life and did not permit me to live my own life. Because he could not abuse me sexually anymore, he was attempting to get back at me.

Just as I thought it was all over, I realized that even though I loved my husband dearly I could never express it physically to the fullest extent. Till date I have never kissed him yet address him as 'Love' and 'Sweetheart'. I am convinced that as I get in touch with my inner issues, the physical healing will be through soon.

Interesting Facts and Findings

It is being accepted more widely that many if not most physical illnesses are actually caused or have their base/origins in emotional disturbances. Ranging from the common cold to Tuberculosis, Jaundice, Cancers, Migraine, Back-ache, Vertigo, etc.

Ulcers for example, it is accepted by Medicine for many long years, are the result of emotional stress and tension.

In our experience, most illnesses have their beginnings or roots in emotional hurts. So much so that even magazines such as TIME and NEWSWEEK have carried cover stories to the effect, predicting that the medical profession in the 21st century will have to treat patients not merely for physical symptoms but for emotional stress and disturbances.

It would seem that whatever goes in, must come out. Emotional hurts pile up one on top of the other, but cannot settle down in "peace". They jingle around in the soul, causing unrest, distractions and sleepless nights. At some point, they break out. Among other ways, the most common would be through the body i.e. through physical sickness. The more serious the sickness such as a cancer, the more serious, severe and intense the emotional hurt.

It seems a convincing fact that, almost every single human being who is physically sick (and who isn't) no matter what the illness, is likely to have a negative emotional root to that illness. Exceptions are not too common though illnesses coming through the genes, commonly known as heredity illnesses, come under a totally different category and might need a whole new book in that area.

Take for example the common cold, which one might accept as inevitable. Ask yourself "What tension, irritation, anxiety or upset did I experience just prior to contracting it?" Secretaries might return home from a hard day of office with a splitting head-ache. Ask yourselves "Why?" Were you loaded with someone else's' work, which you took on with a plastic smile upon the outside but a seething furnace upon the inside. Did last minute demands of your boss prevent you from keeping a date with your son at the ball game, leaving you angry and in a rage?"

Extract of Testimonies:

....I was suffering from cold and sneezing for more than ten years

....Almost instantly I was cured of severe migraine head-aches and a little later of a tennis elbow as well.

....I had the habit of dozing off to sleep, whenever, wherever. Until I located the deepest root hurts in my life and forgave those concerned.

....Around May 3rd I began with severe pain in my back which practically paralyzed me. It looked like another attack of spondulosis or slip disc, which I was familiar with but even after a month of bed rest there was no improvement at all. An MRI showed haemangioma (a bunch of blood vessels) at two places on the D4 and D9 vertebrae. Degeneration and swelling of vertebrae at the lumbar region had taken place. Fluid between the discs had dried and the friction between them gave me pain. Tests at Tata Memorial concluded there was no malignancy and I was asked to return for a check up after three months.

In addition I was found to have a stone, the size of an almond, in the right kidney.

Fr Franklin encouraged me to begin the Forgiveness Therapy. At first I could not forgave certain people but as I progressed I was able to. I realized there were many hurts that I was carrying from the time of my conception. I felt some amount of heat was released from my back. The pain was better but not much. As I progressed with the therapy and went deeper, I was relieved totally and a new joy and inner peace came to me.

Finally a Sonography could not locate any stone anywhere in the kidney. The doctor too, was shocked.

...Through a process of deep Repentance and Forgiveness, I have grown in my self-esteem, been changed in my attitudes towards God and others. Physically too I have experienced many healings such as:

Lichen Planus (a skin ailment) I was suffering from for the past 30 years.

Body ache all over

Pain in both ears for which operations had been scheduled and later cancelled.

Even my eyes were healed and I no longer had to use glasses.

Emotionally and Spiritually I was in darkness, a world of my own with problems and difficulties and sicknesses, always depressed and worried and living in fear, totally rejected, never at peace.

What about accidents such as tripping, loosing your balance, slipping and as a result, cracking a bone. No doubt that the bone that has been fractured or even broken, needs physical attention and treatment. But it is not uncommon that such accidents take place when tensions of the following kind, build up:

- being forced to do something against one's will
- being unsure or doubtful about a decision to be made
- struggling with a mental battle
- worrying about a sick child/patient at home
- worrying about finances and such like

Example 22: A Pastor

At a programme which I had attended was a pastor with one arm. Out of curiosity I enquired how and when it happened. While crossing the road in front of his Church, which was situated on a highway, he slipped, fell and could not avoid a passing truck from running over his arm. When I first enquired whether he had been under tension of any kind prior to the accident, he promptly refuted the same. But over the days as we grew more friendly, he did share the following:

He was the one responsible, for collecting a large burse or fund, for a specific project. He was the principle signatory to the account. His transfer to another parish prevented him from putting those funds to use. But he still remained principal signatory. Then comes the demand from his superior to release the funds for a totally different purpose.

He refused on principle. He was responsible to all the persons who had made contributions to the fund, on his word. This 'unjust' demand from an authority enraged him. He battled it physically, in person, in the emotions and with prayer. However the authorities applied the pressure, assuring him that they were now taking responsibility for the funds collected.

It was during this period of his life, this torment that he was going through, that he met with the accident. This period of his life lasted a good couple of years. To him, he was 'losing control' of the battle, knowing that he would eventually have to give in to authority. This 'losing control' was akin to hurt, feeling insecure, being forced to do something against his will and conscience. On that fateful day he 'lost control' of his footing, slipped and fell.

Hence it is seen that often, in a case of physical illness including the kind mentioned above, there seems to be a starting point, a beginning, an initial cause or root, in the emotions.

Yet we would be in grave error should we make absolute statements. One cannot claim categorically that every case of illness and every form that physical illness takes, must have its roots in negative emotions.

Dealing with emotions to heal the Body

If we accept the findings of psychology... . If we accept that the Physical, Spiritual and Emotional act together as one... . If we accept that the Emotions are the greatest influencing factor in the development of the human person... . Then how much credence do we give, to the effect of negative emotions upon the body, i.e., physical life. *How much are we willing to concede that we need to consider the emotions, before we diagnose and treat?*

In all humility we must try to figure out what effect the negative emotions have had in bringing about the illness. We must try to understand better, their role in the physical condition of the person. We must give them due respect and attention.

Often enough the obvious is bypassed. We do not realize how much a particular situation has affected us, passing it off as nothing. We make light of situations and people, pretending nothing has hurt or effected our composure. We would need to become sensitive and pay more attention to these daily taken-for-granted occasions at home, at work, at church.

Another word for sickness and illness is the word DISEASE. This word however, when broken up like this : DIS - EASE would mean being dis-at-ease in your mind, in your emotions. This dis-at-ease in the mind somehow makes you vulnerable and lowers your resistance to disease in the body. The physical or outer sickness is merely a sign of an inner disease, a sickness in the inner being, the inner self.

Some schools of psychology claim, as much as 80% of all sicknesses are caused by emotional stress. Others go as high as 90 and even 95%. While this might not be an absolute, it gives a fair indication of what we are dealing with.

Hence, in the treatment of illnesses, how much does the medical profession try to treat the emotions? It is my firm belief that if the above principles are accepted, treatment of the hurt emotions will give a lending hand to the treatment of the body. Every now and then, medical findings indicate that the happier a person's disposition, the happier his life, marriage and relationships; the better his health will be, the better he will respond to treatment, the faster his healing will take place.

Example 23: Doris

It was on the 18th of Sept 2006, that I underwent a surgery for Umbilical Hernia. At first I believed it was a minor surgery and I would soon be well again. Contrary to my belief, I found things getting worse. After approximately 2 months, my sutures began discharging and I developed abcesses on the abdomen. Daily dressings were required. This continued for another 8 months. Due to this a repeat surgery was done on the 8th of May. 3 excisions were made at 3 sites on the abdominal wall. The biopsy report indicated I was suffering from Koch [TB] of the abdomen. The doctors then put me on TB drugs.

However even after this treatment the discharge continued and the drugs began having side effects. I developed swellings on my feet, my left foot had turned black and I could not use it any more. I could not even walk now. A blood test was taken and the doctor noticed that all the blood levels like Creatine, uric acid, etc., were very high.

I was referred to another specialist at Hinduja hospital. On examining me with another battery of tests, he concluded that I was not at all suffering from Koch and had been given the wrong treatment. More antibiotics were prescribed for a period of 6 months and I was called for a check up after ten days. A few days after beginning the new set of antibiotics, I began to have severe side effects, I could not retain any food or drink. On my visit to the doctor for a check up, he asked for another round of tests. The reports were quiet bad. He stopped the antibiotics immediately as they were doing me more harm than good. He then washed his hands and said that he could not do anything for me as the medicines were not working on me.

As I returned home I was at a loss. It was now 13 months since the whole of my abdomen was covered with bandages. In desperation I attended the Inner Healing Programme. As I listened to the talks on forgiveness, it dawned on me that I had not forgiven my husband.

Two years into our marriage and our marriage was on the rocks. My husband harassed me constantly, returning home drunk everyday and even beat me. He was without a job and this went on for years. The burden of bringing up my 2 children fell entirely upon me.

I began the process of forgiving my husband by making use of the forgiveness therapy taught to me at the programme. The team supported me even after. After about 15 days I noticed that all the wounds had begun healing. The doctors too were surprised and removed all the dressings. I am now well again.

Other factors at play

Heredity/Genetic

Often an illness has been categorized as 'heredity'. While the medical profession might insist there is nothing one can do about it, it does seem to have two factors worthwhile considering. One could be called the pre-disposing factor, which means, that which comes from the genes, that which is underlying, in the background but quiet and hidden. And the other can be called the triggering factor, which invariably is the emotional hurt. These hurts seem to 'trigger off' what is lying dormant and sleeping. They attack at the weakest point in the body's health system, i.e., the pre-disposing factors. That which was dormant, now comes alive.

Many can testify that allergies to a certain food, or an allergy to the sun, hits in their latter years, for no apparent reason. Much if not most of their lives, they have never experienced the allergy. Science has shown that there might be many alcoholics walking down your street, who have never tasted a drop of alcohol! What then turns them into one, if not the triggering factors that come their way, by way of emotional hurts. Perhaps this will be better understood in the chapter on the Subconscious.

Heart ailments, Diabetes, Alcoholism, Baldness, are some such ailments. Yet dealing with the triggering factors through a process of forgiveness, has brought great relief and in many instances, complete healing. 'Healing of the Family Tree' is a vast new area that has come to light.

The Occult

This is not a new phenomenon. Over centuries, people spanning the continents have indulged in such practices, out of different reasons and motivations. It takes the form of idol worship, tribal-like rituals and beliefs, casting of spells, voodoo, black magic and finally direct satanic worship. It has been observed that physical illnesses can be caused by the power of the occult as well as 'cured' by the same. However this area is purely one that deals with the spiritual and would require a whole different line of treatment. Many publications dealing with this matter, already exist.

The Mystery of Suffering

This is yet another area that can be dealt with by a spiritual faith in God alone. It would imply that suffering is a mystery which may never be explained to its fullest. Sometimes, ailments may fall under this category. Faith would demand an acceptance and wilful resignation to God's Will and plan. However in such cases, the necessary inner peace and strength to look at it in such a way, is usually also granted.

3. How Hurts Affect The Spiritual Life

Now we can attempt to understand how these hurts, like the lava of a Volcano, surge ahead to enter the dimension of the spiritual. Using the same principle that, hurts need to find an exit; in order to affect the physical, they turn outwards to the body. But in order to affect the spiritual, they turn deeper inwards. How can emotional hurts lead us to spiritual sickness, commonly known as

SIN? How can hurt lead us away from God and the relationship we had with Him.

But even before we can attempt to understand this principle, we must acknowledge that for much of the intellectual world, Sin is obsolete. It does not concern many. Sin does not exist. It remains a figment of imagination for the weak, the religious and those spiritual leaders who wish to control their subjects with fear.

If I have become god to myself, who can tell me that anything I do is wrong. If I am free to live my life according to my plan and pattern, nobody is going to impose upon me and interfere with my choice and values. Even for those practising their religious faiths, the awareness of and existence of Sin, no longer puts the 'fear' of God into them.

Example

1. A man has a sexual relationship with a minor. He would be arrested, tried and convicted because a court of law says it is 'illegal' to do so. He would be convicted for breaking a penal law and given due sentence as punishment. But he does not feel guilt for having 'sinned' against a minor. He is not aware or conscious that he has committed a spiritual wrong or offence towards God. He is not conscious of the spiritual harm he has done to himself and the emotional harm he has inflicted upon the minor.

2. The Law in some countries has recognized Abortion, Euthanasia and Same-Sex marriages. This recognition is fast gaining ground in others. But they continue to remain the greatest of sins according to most religions of the world.

3. Spilling of one's seed by masturbating, is considered good and healthy and even encouraged by the medical profession. Christian beliefs consider it an offence to the Creator.

4. The law permits pre-marital sex between consenting adults. In the eyes of God this is Sin. And this would apply for most religious faiths. Some faiths inflict severe punishment and retribution.

Christianity and other religions that deplore these acts, are looked upon with disdain. They are considered to be old-fashioned, dogmatic, behind the times and even a hindrance to growth and freedom. A hindrance to 'finding one's self and reaching one's full potential'. The late Pope John Paul II, while highly respected in death, yet, because he stubbornly stood his ground on many of the above issues, was considered to be a stumbling block to the development of the nations.

The law of the land as against the law of God.

Hence we conclude that for many, they rather respect the laws of the land than the laws of God. And therefore since the laws of 'God' are unpalatable, no longer 'realistic', difficult to maintain, a hindrance to their 'freedom'; they have to become their own god and establish their own rules to life. Notwithstanding the fact that laws change, governments change, policies change. But does God?

Until 1963, it was unthinkable that there should be no prayer in public schools, in the United States of America. A country which until recently still proudly displayed its trust in God, on every dollar bill printed. While the Monarchy of England is represented with the title "Defender of the Faith", Prince Charles has expressed the idea that this title should be changed to "Defender of Faith" to represent the various faiths prevailing in England today. It is not the right or wrong of either case that concerns us, but the change in major policies, thought patterns and stances.

Years ago it was unheard of to legally permit abortion, same sex marriages, adultery, euthanasia, etc. Today these actions are nobody's business but your own. Therefore, who is to say that sex between *consenting* teens, will not become their legal right, in a few years time. Imagine your own child of fourteen, constitutionally and willingly indulging in sexual intimacies, before your very eyes and in your very home.

Or again, who is to say that indulging in sexual intimacies with *consenting* children, will not become legally permissible, in the near future. Imagine it happening to one of your very own darlings. And finally, like the icing on the cake, who is to say that a relationship of incest between father and *consenting* daughter, will not be protected legally?

"Never", you might think. "This could never ever happen. Ours is an educated people, a cultured race, a civilized society. It might take place in another country, another world, but not in mine".

And yet, in your very own country, once upon a time, the activities mentioned above were considered wrong, evil and detrimental to society and children. To tolerate them legally, was unheard of. Today, the very bed-rock of society, i.e., marriage and its definition is under the gauntlet, to make way for legally constituted same sex marriages.

We are gambling on changing ideas, thought patterns and preferences. These ideas begin small, but in time gain momentum and one fine day take center stage. These ideas change from generation to generation, from government to government, from country to country. But the point in question is that God's thoughts, God's ideas, God's understandings, do not and cannot change with time or circumstances. Otherwise, He would not be God!

Here is where you might find yourself on the brink of a precipice. Which would you rather bank on for spiritual security. Which would you consider more dependable, more trustworthy, more lasting. Which weighs heavier in the balance. The Law of the Land or The Law of God. Which would you consider true, presuming of course you would rather live by the truth?

If you decide, out of your convictions, to turn a blind eye to the Law of God, I can have no quarrel with you. But if you genuinely seek Peace, you need to be willing to open yourself to the Truth. *For, only Truth can bring freedom and life.* You need to be willing to shed mental barriers, years of resistance and perhaps even falsehoods you have been lead to believe in. You need to recognize and sift between the suction-like pull of the emotions, and the tough straight-forward objective truths. Refer to Bondages and Obsessions in chapter ten.

New Age Movement

NAM led by gurus from both East and West, has made a clear departure from the traditional concept and idea of God and spirituality. God who is understood and believed to be Person, Creator of all, source of all life and goodness, having a relationship with and authority over man, having power over evil; is now reduced to an energy – a divine cosmic energy. All that exists in material form, be it the universe, man, creatures or nature; is a part and parcel of this divine cosmic energy. There is no more any distinction between Creator and Creation. All is God and God is all. "The universe and I are one". Therefore the belief that I am God and God is me.

What man has to aim for is the blossoming and realization of his full inner self, self-actualization, self-fulfillment. This new spirituality offers an elixir and ecstasy to life, through any means available and comfortable to himself such as free sex, new philosophies, chemicals, yoga, mediums, astral projections etc. in order to achieve a greater union with and into this divine energy. It results in the deification of self, in an awareness that I am god.

All that man may ever need can be found in this energy - knowledge and information, peace and healing, seeking the future and understanding all things, to be self-reliant and deal with every problem. The potential and all answers are within him. There is no need to seek for anything, any help, any guidance, outside this energy. Man becomes self-contained, self-reliant.

No religion is necessary. No spiritual laws are required. Belief in sin and evil is mere theory and untruth. Therefore the need for salvation and mercy is a fairy tale. Man is therefore free to use his life, his mind, his body and his soul in any way he so desires. He needs to answer to no one. He is accountable to no one but himself. He is god. He does not need the God of tradition. No holds barred. He is free.

The question that now arises is Why? Why reject the idea of a personal God and His authority over you, to become a god to yourself. Why the need to be independent and aloof from any form of outside power. Why does one find it so difficult to accept a power, a knowledge, a truth, a wisdom, over that of your own. Why does one need to be all-knowing, all-seeing, all-powerful and 'complete' in oneself?

All indications point to the element and possibly the epitome of pride. Pride can be understood as the extreme and most intensive display of insecurity. An insecurity, that arises due to a weakness in the emotional structure and foundation. An insecurity, that proceeds from an unhappy childhood and possibly, a series of broken homes down the generations. An insecurity, that indicates an absolute loss of anything to hold on to. No base, no foundation, no firm ground to stand upon.

An insecurity so damaging that the only form of self-preservation it can locate, is falling in love with self. Falling in love with one's own beauty, body, power, talents, authority. Protection and indulgence of the self in every way, becomes topmost priority. Raising the self upon a pedestal becomes the crying need of the hour. Deifying the self, provides the acceptance, the acknowledgement, the respect and finally the all-important self-image.

Having established this backdrop, we can now proceed to explain the effect of hurt upon our moral and spiritual values. How hurt can be the cause of sinful actions and sinful ways of living. How hurt can cause us to reject God and turn away from Him.

Firstly, we understand 'SIN' as a reaction, an anger, a wrong-doing towards those who have hurt us.

The Story of Saul and David

In order to understand this principle better, let us take another story from the Bible. Saul and David are two most interesting characters. Saul had been chosen and appointed by God to be King over his people. Saul became very successful and strong. But he also became very heady and proud. More and more Saul would take things into his own hands, disobeying the instructions of his God, doing what he thought was best. For this, God rejected him from being king over his people.

Instead God chose David a little shepherd boy. David used to soothe Saul with his singing and his harp. David grew and began to go out in battle. He would come back victorious from his wars. The women would exult from their windows and courtyards, 'Saul had his thousands but David had his tens of thousands' obviously giving him greater praise, applause and honor, than what was given to Saul.

Saul grew jealous of David, angry that God had chosen this little shepherd boy to replace him, and on one such occasion decided to murder David. He made many attempts to do so, but failed. In fact David would turn the tables over and ask, "Saul my Lord, why do you try to kill me? What have I done to you?" Saul would reply "Nothing" and immediately make another attempt to kill him.

Truly David had done nothing to Saul. David himself, of his own, had not done anything that might have hurt Saul in a direct way. David respected Saul and always continued to hold him in honour. But because Saul experienced rejection at God's hands (the middle circle of the diagram), he nursed this rejection in his heart and dwelt upon it night and day. To rejection was added jealousy, to jealousy was added hatred, which led to the decision to kill (innermost circle).

As long as it remained a feeling of 'rejection' at God's hands, it remained in the emotional category. But as a consequence of nursing it and dwelling upon it, it led to a decision. The decision to kill. This would therefore be understood as 'sin' and going against God's commands and desires.

Hurt when harboured in our hearts, when nursed; when tossed about in the mind looking for answers, looking for a way out, looking for a way to carry out one's anger and revenge, develops into sin. Sin can be defined as that turning away from people and consequently, God. A desire to hit back, to harm persons and God. To prove one's self with harsh words and/or extreme actions.

Secondly, sin could also be blaming God for everything; sickness, death of a loved one, loss of a job, break up of a marriage. One turns away from God, stops attending Church and worship. One cannot any longer take correction, listen to advice, follow his guidelines. One decides to take action, rightly or wrongly. Sin is wrong-doing. You wrong your neighbour and as a result even yourself.

Example 24: Manoj

Manoj is a boy of Hindu descent who had fallen in love with a Catholic girl. She loved her faith and insisted he convert to Christianity. Manoj went regularly for instruction to the Catholic priest. After some time of instruction and getting to know the Christian Faith, these were his words to the priest. "Even if I were not to marry this girl, I would still convert, as I have fallen in love with Jesus".

One day, for some odd reason Manoj had not prepared for his instruction. The priest who was ill that day and, therefore, irritated and vexed, expressed anger and annoyance, literally shouting at him in these words "If you do not take the trouble to prepare, what kind of Christian can you be? Do you really love Jesus or is this merely a ploy to marry your girl friend"?

Manoj was hurt to the core, as you can imagine. If a man of the cloth could behave in such a way and speak such harsh words, what kind of God did he believe in? He left the priest and never returned. By this time of course, he and his girl friend had given their hearts to each other and it was too late to call it off. It was easier to put a halt to the instructions in the Faith and get married in a court of law. And that is exactly what both of them did.

Example 25: Frank Smith

There was the case of Frank Smith (name changed), a well known Telly Evangelist who commanded a wide audience in every continent, a world wide ministry through his audio and video tapes and who brought thousands to the knowledge of Peace. Over night it came crashing down when a couple of American journalists (that's what they are famous for) tracked him down over a span of time, documented his involvement with a woman/women in a brothel and splashed it across every newspaper in the country. All the good he was doing was destroyed overnight with one stroke of the pen.

But let us study Frank Smith. His weakness was obvious to himself. Hidden from the eyes of the world he must have struggled with it in prayer. He was a genuine man. He had a genuine experience of God, a life-changing experience. He was in love with his God and must have known that his habit, his weakness, was sinful and unpleasing to God. He would have prayed, fasted and struggled about it within his own mind and with his councilors. He might have even begged God to heal and save him just as he was able to heal, save and benefit millions of viewers over the world.

But legally speaking he did no wrong. After all it was a matter of two consenting adults, having the freedom to indulge. There was no question of a court case or a ruling about their activities. Why then did the media make such a big issue of it? Why did the media take all that trouble to break him, when he had done nothing wrong legally? Was it because they believed in printing the 'Truth', that one needs to 'practice what one preaches' or that it made an excellent scoop?

Perhaps all he needed to be aware of, was the need of some healing within himself. Probably deep in his subconscious and especially during his formative years he had missed out on a mother's caring and nurturing love. Perhaps through this relationship he was attempting to fill in the gap of a mother who was absent, uncaring or controlling. The 'sin relationship' with a prostitute was an outer sign of this deep inner need. This deep inner need for love as a child, was transposed into his adult-hood now, as the need for the sexual. A little counsel/prayer and the whole story could have ended differently.

100

Examples 34 of Hyacinth and 37 of Pierce, both in chapter 10, helps illustrate this point further.

There are those who turn out greedy and selfish. Others, uncaring and uncompassionate. Pornography, paedophilia, homosexuality, lack of God in people's lives, craving for sexual perversities and gratification, lusting after luxuries and comforts, wealth and power; hatred and jealousy, gossip, slander and abusive language; robbing and lying; all fall under the category of wrong doing and sin. Yet each one of them, as strange as it might seem, can be traced to the need for love. The need for the basic foundations, the need for healing, peace, security and confidence in the emotions.

Let us take a young lad of say 14 who has just been introduced to hard liquor by his companions. It might have one of two effects upon him. If this young lad has a strong foundation of love and emotional bonding, he will be in control of himself and not permit the taste for liquor to overpower him. He will not feel the need for it. As he grows up, he could get used to a drink every evening but he could always be in control.

On the other hand if he has not been the recipient of foundational love, in all likelihood, the taste for liquor could begin to meet that need within and he could very easily become bound by it. And likewise with drugs, smoking, gambling, and the like. Each in its own way has evoked the need within and has become a substitute for that need.

4. How Hurts Effect Our Concept of/Idea of Relationship to God

Psychology is a strong advocate for the argument that, our idea of who God is, what kind of a person he might be, what sort of nature he might have, is directly related to our experience of and relationship with a real life human father. In other words, the vertical is directly influenced and in fact controlled by, the experience of the horizontal.

Little children are often told that God is good. God is kind. God is love. God is your heavenly Father. The conscious mind tries to take in these truths. But the subconscious immediately pricks up its ears when told that God is Father and compares/relates/equalizes heavenly Father with the experience of "DAD" on earth.

An experience of love and kindness from an understanding 'DAD' will leave little to doubt that God is a caring and loving Father to us all. But an experience of domination and strictness, beating and child abuse, drunken orgies and violence, will implant clearly in that child's mind an image that God is hard, reacts with anger and wrath to sin and weaknesses; someone to be afraid of. These notions can dictate one's whole course of life.

Example 26: Michael

Michael came to me saying that in his attempts to grow spiritually, to grow closer to God, he always felt a deep block or gulf between God and himself. He had tried many methods of prayer and meditation; read a number of books on the same and yet felt this terrible 'separateness'. He was longing to experience God's love in a deeper and more tangible way rather than only have an intellectual understanding. He longed to meet God in a personal way and come close up to Him. You could say he wanted to see Him face to face.

The first question I asked him "How was the relationship with your father when you were a child?" stopped him in his tracks and he replied with great disbelief "this is one thing that has always mystified me. The one thing I never managed to fathom. My father is a good man and yet there has always been this distance between us and I have never understood it."

Michael came from a little village where everybody knew the other. His father for reasons of his own hated his own father i.e. Michael's grandfather. The relationship reached such a pitch that one fine day Michael's father left home saying "I never wish to see you again. I wish never to remember you and cut off all dealings with you from today". With this he left home, settled down in another village, got married and Michael was the first born. Michael was born on the feast of the village i.e. St Michael.

The villagers with great joy would say to his father "Ah, a son born on the feast of our patron is a great honour and blessing to your family and the village. You must name him Michael of course". Much to the fellow villagers' surprise his father reacted with scorn and anger, "Never. No he will not be named Michael" Many hours of cajoling and discussions would not make his father budge, nor was any light shed as to why he did not wish his son to be named Michael.

Till, finally they got together as one and threatened to throw him out bodily from the village if he did not consent to their demand. For, not to name the child after the village patron, especially when born on the feast day, would be a terrible insult to the village and the saint. Under great pressure and totally against his will, he was forced to name his child Michael after the patron of the village.

Ever since then his father was never able to pick up his son, into his own arms. Never able to express his fondness, joy and love. Never able to be proud of his son and share his life with him. Why? Because Michael's grandfather's name was also Michael and this boy now reminded his father of the man he hated, the one he never wanted to remember, or think of or see. Ever since Michael's christening, his father was never able to express his love to his son. He was unable to embrace him, play with him, even look at him. In fact, Michael repelled him.

This then is the reason Michael was never able to experience his father's love. This was the block between himself and his father. And this also became the reason for his block between himself and his God. His subconscious made a connection between his experience or rather a lack of an experience, with his father, and his God who he was brought up to believe was 'Father' to him.

While his conscious tried to take in the truth that God was a loving father, the subconscious zeroed in on his *negative experience with his own father. This was why he could not reach into God's presence, this was why he could not feel God's love, this was why he always felt a block, a chasm, a separation from God.*

Others may not be as fortunate or unfortunate as Michael. Many have been physically and emotionally beaten, rejected, dominated and suppressed. Many have grown up without a parents' love, without a secure home, with parents who have been divorced/re-married, in foster homes, in half-way houses, as delinquents or orphaned.

How then can they come to know God as love. How then can they come to experience comfort, peace and security in a God who cares for them. Have they even had an opportunity to be introduced into an atmosphere, which is anywhere near Godly. Have they been given a taste of God's life and times here on this earth? If not from their parents, where then can they expect to receive love and consequent security?

It is no wonder then, that so many are afraid of God. So many doubt his purposes, his intentions, his response to life and action. So many misinterpret the happenings and situations in life, as his punishment and chastisement. So many believe he is a judge whose only job is to pass judgements upon us. Or a policeman whose job is to catch you out when you slip up. Or a puppeteer who pulls the strings and calls the shots totally oblivious and disinterested in the effect upon us and our lives. So many believe that God is far away, cold-hearted like stone, uninterested in our lives.

And finally, having had little or no experience of love, how many cannot even believe in the existence of God. Consequently they have had to and been forced to, establish for themselves, their own theories and philosophies to life; its origins, its purpose and direction. They have had to set up their own standards, their own values, do their own thing.

The only limitation is that their code of life has to be contained within the boundaries of the law of the country they live in. Their beliefs and life patterns, their philosophies and values, have to be submissive to that of the law, established by the land they live in. The law becomes above all, the only rule they need live by.

The philosophy behind this thought pattern can be summarized in these words "you are free to do what you want. No one can tell you what to do or what you should be doing. You are your own boss". In other words, while you have rejected the idea and concept of God, you become *god* to yourself.

5. How Hurts Effect Our Relationship with others

On occasion, the wife and I might have a difference of opinion, which sometimes escalates into a war of words, ending up hurting each other deeply. Yet, we are deeply in love and truly cannot do without the other. Hence, when one such incident takes place, it is as though our hearts are torn out. There remains a terrible emptiness and loneliness. Our lips crack dry and our hearts broken in a pain we cannot describe. The wife has this amazing ability to cut herself off from her hurts and proceed with the daily routine while all the time crying silent tears within. I on the other hand feel strongly and am often paralyzed when such an incident takes place. Unable to do a thing, unable to think or work, I move around like a zombie knowing only the longing to have her in my arms again.

In a way this is what hurt does to everyone. Hurt breaks relationships, cuts one off from the other, destroys anything that is good and beautiful and kind. Hurt kills, ruins and destroys all that is constructive, positive and holy. This is seen especially in the area of family, marriages, children. For this is the basis, this is the nucleus of civilization: The family.

Regrettably, people prefer to let their feelings rule them rather than their mind. They forget the romantic days when they fell in love, the exhilarating moments when hands touched and lips brushed a cheek. The days when they said to each other "You are my only love. I will never give you up until death do us apart". Instead the hurts begin to take over.

These hurt feelings are real, alive and powerful. They chip at the base of the relationship, i.e. the commitment or promise to hold on together through thick and thin, through the virtues of communication, listening, sacrifice and forgiveness. *Erosion takes place.* Bitterness and sadness begin to set in, delusion and loneliness. The couple ends up with divorce due to "Irreconcilable Differences". This too, after years of marriage.

Then comes a new partner on the scene as reported in the newspapers and the media about many of our beloved Rock Stars, Actors and Actresses, and others in the limelight of Show Biz ' What a difference you have made to me. You have changed my life.' This is not an unfamiliar statement.

Can this really be true? Or are we being mislead by our emotions and modern philosophies?

Take the example of the human body. If my little finger is hurting, can the rest of the body keep smiling and dancing or does the whole body feel the pain? A bee sting on the arm will get the whole body hopping and jumping in pain. This takes place for the simple reason that each part of the body is so closely linked to make the whole body. Each part of the body is distinct, has a role to play, yet together all the parts make up the one body.

It would be foolish to imagine the little finger that has been stung by the bee, screaming with pain, while the rest of the body is dancing around, enjoying itself, detached from the pain in the little finger. It would also be foolish to imagine an arm or a leg saying "I am more important. I have other needs and interests, which you cannot cater to. I do not need you, body". So it separates from the body, dangling in mid-air doing its own thing. As foolish and stupid such a thought or imagination is, the same applies to the family.

Each family is called to be one in spirit. Each person in that family is important, connected through blood, joined together in thoughts, ideas, values and spirit. While each would have a special role to play, with unique gifts, talents and abilities; no one can function alone and independent of the others. All are interdependent. The children are not complete without their parent's love and protection and guidance.

The parents are no longer "whole" in themselves because part of themselves have gone to make up their children. Their individual identities are now lost and submitted to that of the family. A child facing difficulties in school etc. will bring concern and a healthy tension to all at home. Dad losing his job will have repercussions on everyone.

How then at any stage of the game can spouses break away saying

"We are no longer compatible"

"I cannot be one with you any longer"

"I do not need you any more"

"We can no longer see eye to eye"

"My career is at stake. I need to go my way."

Example 27: Josephine

Josephine was married and with children, yet felt alone and bereft of family. She felt her own family, i.e., parents, brothers and sisters had rejected her, ostracized her from their love and unity. She felt rejected and alienated.

In truth she was the only daughter of her parents, much loved by all and especially by her father. She was her father's pet. So much so her father would do anything and everything for her, short of spoiling her. She on the other hand could get anything she wanted from him.

One day she interrupted his work like she had done on many occasions before. She was only seven and as before would claim his time and presume his lap was hers, whenever she needed it. But this time her father was engaged with some very important and urgent work and did not wish to be disturbed. This she could not accept or understand because never had he thwarted her before. She persisted in her demands, irritating him and in the attempt to get into his lap, overturned the ink-bottle all over his papers.

He yelled at her with a hard stunning slap on the cheek. With shock and disbelief she left quietly. Her father of all people had struck her. Something totally unimaginable had taken place. She felt a total rejection and ever since felt that the family was rejecting her. She felt alienated and separated from the family not because the family was behaving so, but because she felt and believed so.

This memory remained with her all her life till now at the age of forty plus it came to her vividly and with buckets of tears. Tears that had been suppressed for the major part of her life.

Hurt separates us from one another. Hurts put up barriers in relating. Hurts cause us to avoid those who have hurt us. Hurts break up families, neighbourhoods, and communities. Hurts finally break down society and civilization.

6. How Hurts Affect Job/Work/Business Situations

Example 28: Bismark

Bismark was desperately trying for a job in the Middle East, where remuneration was many times more than at home. He had approached many agencies, was interviewed often and even promised the job. Waiting for the Visa, his passport expired. By the time he received a new passport, the visa would expire and he would have to wait for another. In this fashion he went on for a whole year, needing the Visa, the passport and the no-objection from Police Clearance to fall in line all at the same time. It never seemed to be happening.

He came to me for counsel. I counseled and worked with him for a severe insecurity, arising from a very strict and regimented father, who had controlled his thoughts and actions and personality. His father's influence, expectations and control over him was so great, that he was not really living for himself but for his father, now long dead.

Having counseled him accordingly, he left. I never saw him again till two years later. On inquiry it seems, his papers and visas came through so quickly that within a week he was off to the Gulf. He did not have time to say bye to his friends.

Is this a coincidence? Perhaps to some. And yet such a phenomenon needs to be witnessed to be believed. Others have complained of being superseded at work by those of lower rank or seniority. When the time comes for promotions and increments, they were either skipped by, overlooked or missed the same by a hair's breath.

Others in business will testify that whatever they have touched, whatever they have ventured into, whatever risks they may have taken, have always blown up in their faces finally. That they have been able to grow and establish themselves upto a point but finally all their effort, wisdom, knowledge and expertise in the business, comes crashing down over their heads.

Invariably this kind of experience happens to those who have, as children, gone through forms of criticism, domination, ridicule, suppression, comparison, etc. Some have been told clearly by parents that:

- you will always be a failure
- we curse the day you were born
- you brought bad luck on us, it will follow you always.

What really is happening is that these messages enter from the conscious into the subconscious mind. When young and at the formative age, a child will believe most everything it is told. Thus such a so-called 'curse' or bad omen becomes the truth. The subconscious somehow has to make these 'truths' come to pass. The subconscious being nine times more powerful than the conscious, finds this an easy task. No matter how much you do, you will always be a failure. More about the subconscious, in the next chapters.

7. How Hurts Affect Our Attitudes: Positive and Negative

Another and a final effect of hurt is upon our attitudes towards people and situations. How do we look at others and what inner feelings do we experience towards them. Are we critical, judgmental and in general negative towards others; the things they say, the way they speak, dress and walk. How do we respond or react towards situations? Are we pessimistic, fearsome and underconfident, at a loss?

The following example might shed light on the subject. A group of people listen to your lectures. You point out to them a beautiful scene depicted upon the wall paper on the side wall. It is a scene of nature, with trees and bushes alongside a gentle flowing river. The sky is dotted with birds, butterflies and flying insects.

Most will exclaim at the beauty of the scene and really relish it with occasional oohs and aahs. It will not be strange however, for one person to point at one tiny black spot in a remote corner of the wall paper saying, "But what is that?"

There are those whose eyes and hearts notice the tiny blemishes that mark a beautiful scene, painting, situation and even person. Rather than notice the expanse of beauty all around, their attention will be caught by that tiny blemish. This is the way we are made and generally live our lives. We tend to notice the negative in our neighbours, the tiny frailties in their mannerisms and personalities, rather than the other beautiful characteristics and traits.

In difficult situations perhaps, they might look at the worst thereby passing by wonderful opportunities and occasions to grow. When a suggestion is made by a member of their Executive Team, they will be the first to negate it before even looking at all the possibilities and attributes. Such persons become the thorn in the flesh, the obstacle to growth and development, not only to themselves but to the others they are working with. Such situations eventually end up with fatal solutions.

Hurts received at childhood; lack of constructive criticism, pessimism and such like, leave indelible marks for life and makes one behave and react and look at people and situations in like manner.

Summary

This mind that we have, these emotions that we experience, can they really affect us so drastically? Can they infiltrate every area of the human life and can they really cause so much damage to self and others?

Some would find it more comfortable to ignore and disbelieve them. For others it would take courage to accept and work upon it. If you can accept studies, findings and developments that have taken place in the sciences, in the medical field, in astronomy and oceanography; to complete your knowledge and wisdom you just maybe need to accept the studies and findings that psychology too has made.

But since this refers to our personal lives and the way we run it, we want to have the freedom to make the choices to our likings. We do not wish to be bound by anybody, by any rules, by any restrictions, by any authority. For that matter, we do not wish to be bound even by God. Since most however, might find it too drastic a step to do away with Him completely, we might acknowledge Him, without acceding too much. At any cost, our freedom and free Will must remain free to move in whatever direction we may choose or please. Again, we become 'god' to ourselves.

Wisdom and Maturity would dictate that while freedom is to be respected, there are limits, there are confines within which that freedom is to be operated. Wisdom and maturity would prompt one to realize that our freedom and authority cannot be equal to or likened to that of God. Above all, wisdom and maturity must necessarily caution us that our freedom and authority cannot supersede that of God.

In the final analysis, this becomes a battle between pride and humility. Pride focuses upon the self, while humility focuses upon God.

Chapter Seven

THE TITANIC AND THE ICEBERG

The Titanic was considered at its time to be the world's largest, fastest and most luxurious liner ever to be built. It was considered to be unsinkable; so safe was it that the builders of the liner publicly proclaimed, that even God could not sink it. And yes looking at it one could not but notice its enormity of size, massiveness of proportions, strength and power. On the other hand what one could not see was the vulnerability of its hull and the rest that was below the water line.

The iceberg for itself was merely water, frozen into solid rock. What could be seen was in no way a threat to experienced seamen but what lay below the water line was a curse that sent the famous Titanic to its watery grave.

From this we learn that not everything that looks strong, tough and invincible on the outside is necessarily so. For what lies on the inside and cannot be seen could be weak and vulnerable and collapse at any time. So it is with the human being. Often enough on the outside we display facades of toughness, strength and power, but on the inside could be a totally different kettle of fish, which might crumble at a whisper.

We speak about the human mind or personality, which has two parts to it, the conscious and the subconscious. The play of one upon the other; forming, shaping and influencing the other are phenomena to be studied with interest. Just as the hidden, the unseen, the below-the-surface area of the iceberg ripped through the massiveness of the Titanic, crushing it, destroying it and leading it to its death; the purpose of this chapter is to understand how the subconscious can do the same to us, our lives, our marriages and our families.

The Man Behind The Ten Commandments

In order to study this in detail, once more I borrow from an age old character popularized by Hollywood. Moses of the Ten Commandments. Moses a character from the Holy Bible was deemed to be a fearless prophet, speaking on behalf of God, performing portents and miracles in His name and on His command, a man very close to God.

Yet he had one known flaw in his personality, i.e., a stutter and a stammer. Due to this, he pleaded with God to send someone else in his place to lead his people out of Egypt. God makes a compromise and provided him with a spokesman in Aaron.

Nowhere else in the story is there a mention of this weakness of speech, nowhere at least upto this point. Another passage in the Bible states "he grew up strong in speech and in deed". One would presume thus that all through his childhood, his formative years, his education and training, Moses never experienced any kind of flaw in his speech.

How then, could this stutter and stammer suddenly appear out of the blue and for no apparent reason. He was by then already a grown man. Especially for one who is described as being "strong in speech" which means he was bold, courageous and outspoken. Where then did the answer lie? Curiosity led me to make a study of this Biblical character and what materialized quite amazed me.

The first we hear of his stammering is much later in the story, when God appears to him at the burning bush. Now psychology is very clear. Stammering and stuttering is usually a result of fear. Fear catches one in the throat and stalls/prevents/hinders the free flow of speech, as commonly depicted in the movies or described in a novel. The important point was to locate the source of this fear.

Moses first experienced fear when he attempted to sort out a disagreement between two Hebrew slaves. Their response to him was 'Will you treat us the same as you did the Egyptian soldier the previous night?' The previous day he had seen an

Egyptian soldier ill-treat a Hebrew slave. In his rage at seeing such injustice, Moses killed him. Thinking no one had noticed, he buried the soldier. When now he realized his secret was no longer a secret, fear raced up into his heart and he fled for his life as his punishment would have been certain death.

The questions that arise are: why would Moses, the favourite son of the Pharaoh have reason to be afraid? Could he not have answered or explained away his mistake to the Pharaoh? The movie depicts the Pharaoh as loving Moses more than his own son. Or may be, if he had asked for pardon would not the Pharaoh grant it to him? Finally, if Moses was the strong and brave warrior and statesman that the movie makes him out to be, would he not have faced his death with courage?

But he was afraid. Afraid with a fear so gripping, that he had to flee for his life. How is it that this fear had such great control and influence over his life and decisions? A fear that is not mentioned anywhere thus far.

It would seem that the Hebrews, in discovering his hidden secret, touched a chord, a raw spot, a nerve that was lying deep inside the man. But where did this fear come from? How and when did it get there? The search was on now, for the root cause of this fear. The only other information we have of Moses is in the book of Exodus Chapter I vs. 22 – Chapter 2 vs.10:

> *"Pharaoh then gave his subjects this command: Throw all the boys born to the Hebrews into the river but let all the girls live. Now there was a man of the tribe of Levi who had taken a woman of Levi as his wife. She conceived and gave birth to a son and, seeing what a fine child he was, kept him hidden for three months. When she could hide him no longer, she got a papyrus basket for him; coating it with bitumen and pitch she put the child inside and laid it among the reeds at the river's edge. His sister stood some distance away to see what would happen.*
>
> *Now Pharaoh's daughter went down to bathe in the river, and the girls attending her were walking along by*

the riverside. Among the reeds she noticed the basket, and she sent her maid to fetch it. She opened it and looked, and saw a baby boy, crying; and she was sorry for him. "This is a child of one of the Hebrews" she said. Then the child's sister said to Pharaoh's daughter, "Shall I go and find you a nurse among the Hebrew women to suckle the child for you?" "Yes, go" Pharaoh's daughter said to her; and the girl went off to find the baby's own mother. To her the daughter of Pharaoh said, "Take this child away and suckle it for me. I will see you are paid. So the woman took the child and suckled it. When the child grew up, she brought him to Pharaoh's daughter who treated him like a son; she named him Moses because, she said, 'I drew him out of the water'".

The King had passed an edict to destroy all male children. All the Hebrew slaves knew of this and were therefore living in fear for their sons. The air was riddled with fear and it was in this atmosphere that Moses was conceived and grew in his mother's womb. This fear would have been prevalent for the full nine months he grew in his mother's womb – every moment of it. It would not be surprising therefore if his parents were afraid for their child, should it be a boy.

This theory would tie in perfectly with modern psychology. But just as soon, I had to put it aside another passage in the bible says, "his parents were people of faith and defied the royal edict". This would indicate therefore that they were not afraid. The fact that they hid Moses for three months implies that they were perhaps waiting for the opportune moment to initiate their plan.

But what did it mean for a three month old baby, in a basket, floating down the river, alone. Until then, I had this pretty image of a basket wrapped neatly and colorfully, serenely sailing down the river, the gentle breeze pushing it along, with the cooing of the birds and butterflies accompanying it.

Little did I realize what it must have meant to him. When the

Pharaoh's daughter opened the basket, the baby was crying! It could be natural, out of hunger or having messed up. But could it also be due to fear - of not being in familiar surroundings, of not having the comforting arms of his mother around him, of seeing and hearing strange people and voices, of not knowing where he was, where he was going, a fear of death? Could it be a rejection or a fear of rejection from his parents?

Here now comes an even more interesting idea. Moses never experienced this in a conscious way. He could never ever be aware of this or remember this because he was too young. There was no way he could ever know what lay therein. It was not even indented upon his subconscious. It was something lying even deeper i.e. in his unconscious.

Were these experiences dead after so many years? Had they frayed away and been wiped out for good, after so many years? Were they no longer of any consequence? Was time a healer to his hurting memories?

No, they lay there in full form, not decreased or subdued in any way, for once there, how could they be reduced or removed? They lay dormant like a volcano, waiting for the opportune moment to erupt in full force, to reveal their true form and colours. All his years as a lad and a young man in the Pharaoh's home, never once was there any indication that these experiences existed within him. Never a tell-tale sign until that fateful day which changed the course of his life.

Conscious and Subconscious

And so it is with us. Every moment of our existence, from the time of conception within mother's womb, is filled with experiences i.e. feelings and emotions; some good and others not so good. Every moment of our existence is recorded in the memory, be it conscious, subconscious or unconscious. Nothing gets by the memory.

These experiences enter through the five senses of Touch, Taste, Smell, Sight and Hearing. Every tone of voice heard, every scary face seen, every rough touch experienced etc. is embossed and nothing can erase the effects of these memories. Hence hurts, fears, insecurities, rejections, suppressions, anger, tensions etc are all recorded for life.

The tenderest ones, the most destructive ones, the most hurtful ones, usually settle down into the remotest and deepest levels of the mind, without us even knowing that they are there. At the right time, when all factors join together and the atmosphere or circumstances are conducive, these hurts lying deep within are triggered off. One then begins to wonder why and how the person reacts so strongly, or behaves in such an irrational way.

What for instance has made you the angry hot-tempered person that you are? Why are you afraid of the night, or of being alone, or of closed rooms, or of heights, or of dogs, or of water etc.? Why are you always shouting and screaming at your spouse and children? Why are you dominating by nature? Or why are you timid and unable to hold your own?

Or again, why the need to indulge in sexual perversities? Why the emptiness and hopelessness, despite a wonderful wife and family? Why divorce and re-marriage? Why do children turn offensive and hostile, despite "providing them with every good thing"? And the questions can go on and on.

Finally, why rebellion at the very thought or idea of a God who is in control? Why the need to take His place?

Like the iceberg, psychology says, the conscious mind is roughly 10 per cent of the whole self and the balance 90 per cent constitutes the subconscious. In other words the subconscious commands a larger area and volume and is nine times more powerful than the conscious. This provides much food for thought.

To make it more realistic, organize a tug of war, with one strong man on one side, and nine other normal healthy men holding the rope on the other. At the word go when each side begins pulling, which side is going to win? You can guess the results in advance.

The word 'Conscious' refers to our awareness level.

Therefore the conscious mind refers to our knowledge, that part of our life that we are in touch with, aware of and can see; our behaviour patterns, our relationships, our strengths and weaknesses, our ability to reason and analyze, to put matter together, to discuss and sift out information, to make decisions and such like.

The word 'Subconscious' refers to that part of our life that is below awareness level. In other words that part we cannot see, we are not aware of or in touch with, we do not understand. For all practical purposes we do not know what lies therein and yet because it constitutes a much larger force/power than the conscious mind, this part of us controls the rest of our life.

For example though we may believe the decisions we have made are objective and balanced, we have no idea of the extent to which those decisions have been controlled and even manipulated by the subconscious. If we can only understand the enormity of what we are saying, it stands to reason that one must and should make it a point to look into these areas of life lying deep below, somehow, by hook or by crook, in order to live life to the fullest.

The subconscious can also be compared to a computer that is programmed to behave in a certain way. The subconscious is programmed from early childhood such that today, as an adult, one behaves, reacts, lives and answers, in a set way or pattern. The subconscious ends up trained to behave and react or respond in a certain way.

For example, fear of an authority figure such as the boss in office would indicate a similar fear of a parent or elder in one's childhood. Having grown up in fear, one is trained and programmed to experience fear in similar circumstances. The subconscious thus sees the parent or elder, in that boss.

The forces that tend to pull, push and influence, invariably seem to win the victory. Keeping in mind the truth that the subconscious is nine times more powerful than the conscious. Many, if not most of the cases mentioned earlier, clearly indicate how past root hurts buried in the subconscious are today the controlling factor in these person's lives. They indicate how by dealing with them they have been set free from the effect of these memories and hurts.

Applications

The subconscious is the greater part of the human person. It automatically has the greater role to play, the more effective and the more powerful influence. What lies therein is unimaginable. There lies the power to make, the power to break, the power to shape and to build. The applications and the examples could go on without end.

The person you are today, the bad habits or weakness in your personality, your values and priorities, the problems you face in marriage and other relationships, your physical illnesses too; can all be traced back to roots lying within the territory of the subconscious.

Identifying them, understanding them and their effect upon your psyche i.e. how your mind has been affected and programmed, is the first major step. It is crucial to first understand how your mind has been influenced, how your attitudes have developed, what controls your behaviour patterns.

Why for example are you a loner and cannot work in a team with others. How is it that fear rules your decisions and your relationships. Why are you a dominating, angry and self-willed father and husband at home. What makes you homosexual. Why are you obsessed sexually with little children. This is the difficult part at first.

The second part, which is also difficult but now becomes easier, is the handling of those memories, hurts and issues not yet resolved. This is dealt with later.

Example 29: Diedre

Deirdre a pretty young lady was carrying a hunch upon her back. I asked her to recollect what could be the possible root hurt causing this hunch. She came back after a couple of days with this story. As a little child of six she contracted a

119

fever, which lasted an unusually long time. The Doctor wanted a blood sample. Now Diedre, because of an even earlier emotional wound, which had resulted in a fear of blood, refused to accompany her mother to the hospital for the removal of a blood sample. She was so adamant and stubborn that the Doctor consented to come to the house.

Even in the house she refused point blank, to stretch out her hand to give the blood sample, which involved a slight needle prick and the obvious sight of blood. In their attempts to hold her down, she riggled out of their grasp and ran all through the house. She remembers even struggling out of the Doctor's grasp and crawling from under his legs to a different corner of the house. But she couldn't do this forever and soon she was held down firmly, her mother literally sitting on top of her while the Doctor removed the blood sample.

She remembers that at that moment her Will finally caved in. Till then she had fought tooth and nail but soon she was totally overpowered. She could resist no longer. With great sadness, fear and despair, she gave in. This we came to understand was the cause of her hunch. Notice anyone who is sad and lost and alone, they invariably walk or sit with head drooping, shoulders sagging and back raised. The hunch of despair first began in the mind and the emotions, and was later expressed or brought out in the physical, i.e., the body.

Having understood how her mind had been affected by that particular event, doing the therapy for healing became much simpler and effective. First however, the memory had to surface from the subconscious where it had been lying dormant for many years, as described above.

Years later when I asked Diedre to write in her own way and words, her story. This is what she replied:

"My memories had just been washed away. It was, to me,

a reminder of the power of forgiveness to heal and make whole. You wrote of how I could put my feelings and thoughts down in a testimony, but there were no thoughts and feelings to put down. When your second letter mentioned the blood test I had had, it was like reading about something that happened to someone else. (You will be glad to hear that when I have a blood test now, even from the vein, I do not even flinch.) Part of it may be just the passage of time (a couple of decades), but time by itself could not heal and bring forgetfulness."

When true healing takes place, the hurt attached to the memory is healed. The memory no longer remains hurtful, distasteful, unpleasant, and slowly slips into the subconscious. That is why for her it felt strange to recall it and write it down. It felt so strange, it was almost that it had never happened to her, that it was someone else's story.

Example 30: Frances

Frances also was an example of a pretty young lady, smart in her dress, intelligent and alert, with a number of other good homely qualities and traits. But she hated herself, always compared herself to others and thought she was useless and of no value. Among many very deep emotional wounds she has experienced there was one that stuck out like a sore thumb, which we began to address.

Frances was born a left-handed person. In those days parents and teachers alike were ignorant of the fact that left-handed persons were usually exceptional in intelligence and creativity. It was her kindergarten teacher who began the trauma by compelling Frances to change from being left-handed to become right-handed.

She would berate her in front of the class, beat her knuckles with a ruler, and daily remind her that left-handed persons were useless, failures and stupid. She even sent a note home to her parents who in their ignorance continued the teachers chastisement at home. She was forced to become a right-handed person.

What in effect did such an action accomplish in Frances. In effect, by forcing her to change and become a right-handed person, she was being forced to change her whole personality. What came natural to her, what she was comfortable with, what was 'her' in the real sense; was being unaccepted, rejected, neglected and disliked. Being so young i.e. about four years of age, it left scars and traumas too deep for words. She was forced to become something she was not, she was forced to be somebody she was not. Her insides, her real self, had the effect of being torn out, twisted and re-set by human hands.

The young mind began to believe that to carry on being what she was, meant to be an evil, dirty, unacceptable person. She began to hate herself for who she was and was never able to see the good things about herself, which we tried so hard to convince her about. It took us three years to bring about some semblance of healing in this child. Today she is married and a happy mother. Where she resides, she is able to help others who have been hurt emotionally.

For Frances, while she could remember this experience quite easily, she had absolutely no idea of the impact it had had upon her. She was not in touch with the feelings connected with that hurt. For her, the hurt feelings were lying deep within the subconscious and were realized or came to the surface only as she began the process of recollecting, more and more.

Example 31: Oscar

The only reason why Oscar came to our programme was because his wife had requested him, hoping things might change for the better. Hence his heart and soul was not in the programme. However during the session of 'Healing of Memories', a memory hit him like a bolt of lightening. His life changed totally. This is what he shared later.

He was in a regular school at the age of eight, doing well and had plenty of friends. His father being business-minded shifted him to another school where the children belonged to wealthy business families. His father had hoped that Oscar would be influenced by these children and their environment and grow therefore to be more like them, business-minded.

But Oscar resented this change of schools because it meant being deprived of friends and surroundings that gave him his security and confidence. He cried daily, refused to get used to the change and demanded his old school and friends back. After some duration his father relented, more out of defeat than anything else, and retracted on his decision.

Oscar went through school and life as any other person might, but took a liking for the liquor bottle. He and his friends would spend the late hours of the night drinking. Mind you, Oscar did not become alcoholic by any means, but this attachment to the bottle and his club friends, caused a vacuum in the relationship with his wife. Often she found herself waiting for hours on end to eat supper with him. Irritated and angry, she would find herself eating a cold and lonely supper. All her attempts to change her husband failed.

Sending him for the programme was the best thing she could ever have done for him. When the memory hit him, after some forty years, he went through a process of forgiving his father. His life changed, he gave up his drinking habits, he realized that his wife was first and most important, and today he is helping the community in a great way.

The point of this example is that a single memory, a single incident and moment of hurt, can cause an upheaval in one's life and ruin marriage and family. One needs to recognize its effect upon one self and necessarily deal with it.

The subconscious is like a prankster. It is always playing tricks on you. When you think you have understood or caught a hold of him, it suddenly pops up elsewhere. It pokes and prods. Now it may be the memory that needs to be brought to the surface, now it may be the negative feelings attached to that memory.

At one occasion the subconscious is so influenced by the hurts, that your mind is led to believe in the effects, causing you to give in to them. On another occasion it makes you fight the hurt feelings, refusing to bow down to them. Hence it is not an easy matter dealing with the subconscious. Like a dream in the middle of the night, the subconscious also needs to be interpreted and understood.

The deepest level of these hidden hurts is now the unconscious. There are incidents and occasions in your life that you have no way of knowing and remembering, either because you were far too young (from the moment of conception until the age of memory) or due to accidents, operations and other such incidents, which rendered you unconscious. But there are ways of getting to these areas and memories of one's life, as we shall see in the following chapters.

The Talking Cactus

My brother loves to recount this story:

"As children and during our summer vacations we would love to visit our Mother's home in a small town far way, called Kanpur. Being the children of the only sister, we would be spoiled rotten. One of the uncles who loved his garden and especially his cactus plants, one day called me aside and showed me what he called the Talking Cactus. On one of its massive fleshy leaves was written, carved out in big bold letters the words 'Welcome Franklin'. This was my uncle's way of saying that he loved me."

What in effect he had done was this: When that particular leaf was young and tender, he had carved those letters into that leaf in very tiny print. By the time of our next visit, the leaf and its imprint had grown large.

What I learned from this quaint little story was that when young, hurts can be easily engraved into our little hearts and minds. As children we are tender, impressionable and malleable. As children we get easily influenced and affected, positively or negatively. We tend to believe everything we are told and experience, as if it were the truth. They may look very tiny and insignificant but over the years especially by the time of our adulthood and particularly marriage, these hurts grow enormously. Or at least their effects upon us and our lives, are very real and powerful.

Can we therefore presume that whatever has happened in our life as children, have a greater influence and power over us, as adults? Maybe this might help to explain why some people are so very cruel, harsh, wicked and evil. Sometimes we wonder how people could reach such extents of depravity. We ask why others cannot control themselves in their irrational behaviour patterns and behave as normal decent persons. Why does one become a terrorist, a Hitler or a Saddam Hussein.

Saddam for example was four months in his mother's womb when his father died of cancer and a few months older when he lost his twelve year old brother to the same. His mother distraught with grief and bitterness, attempted to abort him and kill herself, but failed at both. When born, she refused to have anything to do with him, hence he was looked after by an uncle, until the age of three. His mother married again after which he was reconciled with her. However until the age of 8-9 he was abused emotionally and psychologically by his step-father.

Behavioural analyists explain that, what Saddam went through, was a total rejection and hatred of self. As a means of self-survival, he fell in love with himself to become one of the world's worst dictators.

The subconscious has many more hidden secrets lying therein than we can even imagine. Secrets that have far-reaching consequences.

Chapter Eight

CONCLUSIONS DRAWN

1. PHYSICAL, SPIRITUAL, EMOTIONAL - are three separate and distinct aspects of human life and yet so closely interwoven, that together they make the complete human person. They were created for each other to be one united whole. None can exist and function apart from the others. They work together. At no time can one say "Look here, now I want to live only my physical life; spiritual and emotional, stay out of it". The statement is just as ridiculous as the thought. And yet each is distinct, with a unique role to play.

The science of healing has specialized to such a high degree that you have Medicine that takes care of the body and its physical life only; and you have religious beliefs that take care of the soul/spirit and its spiritual life only; and you have psychology that takes care of the emotional and mental care of persons only. *Perhaps over the years this has become one of man's greatest follies.*

It is heartening to hear that more and more, there is a consensus and union of thought that, the three are actually one. Yes, for example, germs and bacteria and viruses do cause physical illness in a direct way. However, hurt emotions and spiritual sickness such as unforgiveness and sin, are often the underlying link and openings that lead to physical illness. The world is realizing that a holistic approach to medicine is required. The whole person needs to be treated, not merely his human physical body.

2. THE FORMATIVE YEARS - Psychology describes the first seven/eight/nine years as the formative years of one's life.

Hurts described in chapter five under the title An Exercise, are the kind that can take place in this age group. The basic principle remains that, whatever happens until this age, forms and shapes one for the rest of one's life, be it positive or negative. These are the moulding years, the setting years, the 'programming' years of one's life. Personalities are formed, behavior patterns are shaped, attitudes are decided, actions are controlled, and relationships are ruled.

Look at it from another angle, that of the present times. You are an adult, set in your ways; with a certain type of character and behavior pattern, your own peculiar attitude and philosophy to life, your special kind of values and relationships. You have become what you are today because of all that has been fed into you during your formative years i.e. the first nine months in mother's womb and the next nine years of childhood. Should you be a disagreeable person to live with, dominating by nature, or an anxious and nervous type; you know where to look to find the answer and to initiate your healing.

3.   EMOTIONS,   DECIDEDLY,   THE   MOST POWERFULLY INFLUENCING FACTOR in the shaping of the human person. These emotions shape not only personalities and characteristics but even have influence upon the physical characteristics of the child. We look to medical science to explain the reasons for heredity illnesses, deformities in bone structures, mongoloid infants and those born with a hole in the heart.

And yet who is to know what role negative emotions play in such cases. How many of these children were wanted even before their deformities were detected. How many were subjected to stress and traumas of the parents. How many were "abortion attempted" children? An opportunity to meet parents of such physically and mentally deformed children, revealed that in every single case, there were massive amounts of rejection, trauma, hurt, of one kind or the other.

4. FOUNDATIONS Any building or structure needs to have solid foundations on which to rest and stand tall. Likewise a bridge over a river needs to have pillars rooted in strong foundations that can face the vagaries of weather conditions, tides and erosion. Such foundations provide strength and security and allow that bridge or structure to stand erect and strong for many years to come.

In the same way every human life, for it to run smoothly, for it to contribute to society and bear fruit, must be embedded in foundations that provide security, strength, confidence and health. The following can be considered to be the foundation pillars, the basic and intrinsic emotional needs to every human life.

a) Acceptance. Every child needs to be accepted without condition. It needs to feel that acceptance from the moment it is conceived in its mothers womb, to the rest of its life. Whatever may be its gender, colour, features, characteristics and vocational calling; it needs to be accepted. This regrettably is the hardest thing to do, for any parent.

The parent or parents, right at its inception are either not prepared for the child, or want a particular gender, or subject it to the pressures they go through. They begin to make differences, compare and have high expectations for the child. They want the child to be the person they have in mind for it to become, instead of recognizing that it is unique and different in every way. Each child is called to be free, special, gifted, talented and contribute to life accordingly. They are not meant to play the piano because mummy can tell her friends and relatives so, or join the junior basketball league because dad used to play in his days.

In ways big and small, direct and subtle, parents and others begin shaping their child to conform to the picture they have painted. Little do people realize the horrific impact that this can have upon their child. Acceptance is the primary need of every human child, the root to all happiness, the base to wholeness and confidence. And yet it is the most lacking in humanity and in the world. The child either feels accepted, loved and wanted, or rejected, inferior and not-upto-the-mark.

b) Appreciation. An offshoot to acceptance and a building upon that acceptance, is the need to give kudos to the child. To appreciate and praise the child correctly without indulging it, is the second most important foundation or pillar. To give praise where due, builds up confidence and self-worth. Regrettably, appreciation is not forthcoming and this makes the child feel/ believe that there is nothing good in him/her to be recognized, appreciated and counted. No matter how much effort that child might put into the project, somehow he/she does not seem to get the recognition it might deserve/need from the elders. He/she does not reach up to their expectation. This is a sure way of damaging his/her ego and self-confidence.

E.g. When my littlest was two years old, because the other two liked to draw and colour and he did not want to be left out, he would come up to me demanding "Dada, paper". I would oblige. Next he would demand "Dada, colour". I would have to provide him with a crayon. The next moments would see him drawing and colouring furiously what to an adult mind would be a god-awful messy scribble. After some moments of intense concentration he would call "Dada look"!

Was my reaction to be 'You silly child, what a mess you have made' it would have broken him. But I would always blurt out in great wonder and praise "Wow, fantastic". By this I have identified with him, encouraged him to express his feelings and his artistic talent and used that moment as a gentle and loving communication with him. Should I be very busy at that moment and not want to be interrupted, I would say "You must show mama this lovely colouring". Off he goes to show his mother. I have got rid of him without hurting him.

Every one of us needs kudos and appreciation. Every one of us even as adults want to be appreciated for the job we have done, for the roast beef cooked, for the way we have handled the dispute, for the speech given. Often enough we take others for granted and forget these basic and simple requirements, which can go a long way in developing relationships, trust and love.

c) **Respect and Honour.** Not uncommon are times when out of irritation, anger or fatigue I will raise my hand on my sons, not taking the trouble to listen to them or pay attention to what they are saying, feeling and needing. Knowing I have hurt them, I always make it a point to heal the hurt by apologizing and asking their pardon and forgiveness. By this I am conveying to them that they are important persons, worthy of respect and honour. I have no right to throw them around, merely because of my authority and power. They too will grow in respecting and honouring others. They will be able to feel good about themselves as a result.

Correcting children for wrong doing, chastizing them and even punishing them needs to be done in love. That would have a totally different effect upon them than correcting in reactive anger, irritation or impatience.

d) **Love.** Love is a vague and all-encompassing attribute. It would include the above three and so much more such as caring, understanding, forgiving, communicating, patience, kindness, gentleness, etc. Acceptance in its basic and true form is love. The greatest and most difficult form of love is to accept another as is, unconditionally.

It was this kind of love that changed Zacchaeus. It was this kind of love that touched the deepest need in his heart and healed him. He no longer needed to make undue and unjust demands to meet those needs we have already analysed. Instead, he became aware of his wrong doings and promised to correct them.

Love as commonly described by a myriad of authors, is a decision. This is one decision that one can never turn back on.

e) **Positive Self Image.** While this basic emotional need acts as the fifth pillar on which the foundation is laid, it also becomes a consequence of the four already mentioned. The result of having the first four to bank upon is believing in oneself, feeling good about the self in a positive way, aware and believing that one is important and worthy. One is therefore operating from a base of security and strength. Consequently one can also think of and behave towards others in a positive, assuring and encouraging manner.

How few have a positive and healthy self-image. How few truly think well of themselves and can do the same to others. How few can respond positively towards people and situations. How few therefore have a peace in their hearts that everything in this world cannot provide.

5. SECURITY. In the final analysis, what is the foremost need of child and adult is security. Security is the result of the above. Security comes from a stable marriage, a stable job, stable finances and stable parenting. Good parenting must always and necessarily result in 'security'. True security does not come from a room full of toys, every possible kind of candy, indulging the self or the most expensive clothing.

This might only satisfy the desires of the outer 'flesh' or 'carnal desires'. But what about the inner spirit, the inner self. What about the need for caring, sharing, discipline and understanding. True security comes from stability in the parents relationship, stability in the way they bring up and discipline the child.

This does not mean that problems should and will never take place. Of course there will be situations that lead to tension- filled days: situations that test mum and dad's commitment to each other and the child. But when the child is a witness to the way mum and dad handle those situations; when the child sees that both of them together work it out without blaming each other; and especially when it all ends up with a hug and smile, the child knows it can trust.

The child is a witness to parents taking time off to communicate and understand; senses peace when mum and dad have forgiven each other, knows that mum and dad are together in their decision-making and disciplining. Then the child knows that it can always depend on mum and dad. Every need and challenge will be taken care of because dad and mum are always there for 'me'.

The sad truth is that because divorce has become so common place, even before it can actually happen (and may be it won't) children are already fearing the same. Surely they share and discuss among themselves about parents and foster homes. Maybe they even begin to believe that divorce, separation and foster homes, are the normal way that families and marriages have to go. This by itself brings about the most serious kind of insecurity wondering how long their family is going to last.

True security for a couple, lies in knowing that each is going to be faithful and true to the other and not having to worry how long the marriage is going to last. True security for the child, is in knowing that Mum and Dad are his own and he is theirs. Security of this nature brings a quite and confident strength.

6. DYNAMICS OF HURT. Hurts, though negative, have their own specific dynamism, thrust and energy.

i) *Causes a vacuum.* Hurt results in wounds that need to be healed. These wounds are created as a result of an inadequacy of a basic emotional foundation. A weakness in the formation structure. This results in an emptiness, a depravation, a void. This void or emptiness demands to be filled. This void is like a vacuum that sucks in everything to quench the urgent, excruciating thirst for acceptance, attention, love, a positive and healthy self-image. The subconscious tries desperately to fill that vacuum and emptiness with whatever comes its way, unable to and not using reason or objectivity.

ii) *Behaviour. Health. Rebellion.* The result is negative character traits; wrong-doing; 'sinful' actions, life patterns, attitudes; physical ailments; rebellion against any kind of authority. These and many more avenues are explored by the conscious and the subconscious, to fill in the vacuum, to quench the thirsting emptiness, as explored in the previous chapters. One example is 'Health Consciousness' which is the 'IN THING' today. People are ready to do anything, to go to any lengths to keep good health. 'Health' becomes a little 'god'.

iii) *To prove oneself.* Hurt, Wounds, Emptiness, leave a need to be accepted and appreciated, to be recognized as someone who is worthy of respect and honour. The final result is a poor self-image, a poor self-worth. One's true identity is damaged, is lost. In an attempt to compensate for this emotional poverty, one needs to prove oneself. One needs to prove oneself through argumentativeness, controversy, rebelliousness, domination, dress code, indecent language, negativity, thought patterns, weird ideas, weirder behaviour, and so much more.

iv) *Selfishness.* Psychology describes a new-born child as being the most 'selfish' creature upon this earth. For the understandable reason that it can do nothing for itself. It expects every need will be met, demands everything to survive and does not lift a hand to help itself or rather, cannot. It is the center of attraction and has everyone running around it. And this is natural and normal.

Now, suppose (and this is the reality we are speaking about) this child has for one or more reasons, been deprived of acceptance, or appreciation and respect, or honour and love; in other words has a vacuum and emptiness deep within. That child now adult, must and will move heaven and earth to satiate the demands from within. It will not stop at anything to quench that thirst.

The emotional vacuum, therefore, the need to prove oneself and this all-pervading selfishness, this three-in-one factor is the one underlying force and motive that drives us. Selfishness is at the base of this thirsting need to be free and independent. This explains the strongest drive to put our individual interests and concerns first. The 'I' and the 'self' take priority and first place. Intellectual justifications follow, to explain away one's actions, behaviour and decisions. But in the end, it all boils down to plain and simple selfishness.

Every example described, has traces of all the above elements in them. The vacuum, like a black hole, sucks in anything and everything. The poor self-image, that is always trying to prove itself, in order to meet up with standards and expectations, in order to gain attention and acceptance. The selfishness, knowing no bounds, racing to gratify and satisfy those deep inner longings and thirstings.

In our selfishness we can think only of ourselves, our needs, our wants, our freedom. The 'I' comes first, first before others, first before spouse, first before children. 'I' often enough becomes 'god'. And when we decide to become god to ourselves, we become the epitome of selfishness. The epitome of pride. We live in an epitome of deception.

7. A THEOREM. A New-born has to separate from two whole persons in order to become another complete whole.

Obviously, one might say. A simple fact of life, that needs little explanation. A principle, extensively dealt with by psychology over the years, this being the normal pattern of life that every person has to go through.

And yet, easier said than done. In fact, accomplished in a very very few people of this world, possibly less than 2 per cent. This principle is much easier applied to animals than to humans. A newly born calf or foal requires but a couple of hours if not less, to begin prancing around and following its mother. Separating from its mother and becoming an independent whole is comparatively a short time process.

But for humans, it is a very slow and gradual process of leaving mother and father, not merely physically, but emotionally as well. This begins with the cutting of the umbilical cord and continues over a period of a number of years. The child, nurtured and comforted by love, is encouraged to explore beyond its moorings, more and more; developing physically, emotionally and mentally too. Until reaching full maturity he/she is now eager to begin a family of his/her own, beginning the whole process again.

Sadly, this process is jinxed, often enough right from the beginning. Hurt, in its myriad of forms, as we have seen, leaves an empty void and self-centeredness. The person, rather than

134

becoming confident and generative in his creative giving, expends much of his energy and time, attempting to fill in this void. He gets hooked onto sex, chemicals, work, success, power, the limelight etc. With these and more, he attempts to fill in the void, the gaps, the cracks in his basic foundations.

All his life he remains at the level of self: self-seeking, self-grandeur, self-satisfaction. In other words, he remains at the level of the child within him. In truth, he never really grows up. He never really develops emotionally and mentally. He never reaches that stage of creative giving. He is not equipped to function as a complete whole. While the physical umbilical cord may have been snapped at birth, the emotional one ties him down and binds him for life.

This is accentuated if the two who have given life to this person, are themselves broken and crushed due to their own childhood backgrounds and hurts. Deprived of love, deprived of the basic foundation of life, they cannot give what they do not have. If the biological parents themselves are lacking in mother/father's love, they have not grown to be full and complete in themselves. Their emotional umbilical cords could not yet have been snapped and consequently drag them into a bind. They are unable to provide the basic foundation to the life they create.

Phenomena such as over-possessiveness, over-attachment, over-control and protectiveness of any sort; are clear indications by their very terms, that forbid such persons from growing into a complete whole. Time is not a healer. Time does not forget. Time does not set one free automatically. For life, such persons remain under the undue and unnatural influence of their peers. They have not been allowed the freedom to become independent, adventurous and even to make mistakes. In other words they have been prevented from growing physically, emotionally and mentally mature.

Success at work and business is deceptively translated into maturity and growth.

Chapter Nine

GETTING TO THE HEART
OF THINGS

In the first part of this book we have at length dealt with emotional hurt, its effect upon every aspect of our lives, family and community. Finally we saw the effect of the powerful subconscious and the role it plays in manipulating and controlling us. In this half of the book we want to look at some ways of dealing with these hurts in the conscious and subconscious so that we can look forward to healing and wholeness.

Before we can do that, we need to know ourselves well, we need to identify the root areas of hurt, we need to get to the bottom of things. The more we can understand our physical ailments, our behaviour patterns, our spiritual inclinations; the easier to grow into healing and wholeness. The more we can make the connection between what is going on presently in our life and the root hurt from our childhood, the easier and quicker will be the healing. When we can figure out the more than one way in which a deep root can affect us, the better will be our disposition to healing.

In identifying these hurts:

i) we make a list of all those persons who are/were responsible for those hurts, consciously or inadvertently.

ii) We become aware of the effect these hurts have had upon us. We get in touch with the negative feelings attached to these hurtful memories.

iii) Then we proceed to the process of healing and forgiveness, as we shall see in subsequent chapters.

Hence certain points will be repetitive, but this time in a very direct and personal way. This will be done on two levels, the level of the conscious and that of the subconscious.

THE CONSCIOUS LEVEL
What we can remember/recall

Hurts before the age of six

There are those who are just not able to recall childhood memories. This in itself is a pointer to the fact that childhood was probably so painful, they do not wish to remember and recall the same. Much patient counseling is required for such persons. Gradually memories surface and can then be dealt with.

For most others, you need to travel back into your memory, as far back as your mind will take you. Obviously you will not be able to recall every single detail about your childhood leave alone every single hurting experience. But the ones you do recall will probably be the ones having the greatest and lasting impact upon you. The following hints might assist you to know yourself better:

- if parents and others treated you with neglect, scorn, indifference. You consciously missed them and their attention. They were caught up with friends and parties and left you in the hands of the baby-sitter. Their careers and social life came before you. They had no time for you.

- You were corrected with harshness and made to feel stupid, ignorant, a good-for-nothing. You were humiliated in front of others and picked upon unjustly. The neighbours poked fun and embarrassed you, while dad and mum said nothing.

- You remember the bitter quarrels your parents used to have and how you felt. Dad had a weakness for the bottle and Mum for nagging.

- They seemed to prefer the others, or the boys, or the girls. You felt you were a misfit, a mistake, an afterthought.

- Your first day at school was a calamity. You felt totally abandoned by mum and dad as they waved good-bye. They were late in dropping you to school and picking you up, leaving you at the mercy of others.

- You were compared with others and criticized for your looks, dress, complexion and intelligence.

- Sexual abuse at the hands of neighbours, teachers, older children or incest from a family member are most maiming and degrading.

- Fear of the dark, of being left alone, of harsh and alcoholic parents, of animals, of thunder, etc.

- Trauma arising from accidents, near-drowning mishaps, surgery.

Be aware of these hurtful memories and fears, become aware of how you feel, how they have affected you over the years and today. *It is important to relive these feelings and allow them to surface.* You could feel abandoned, rejected, unloved, insecure, lacking in confidence, guilt feelings, fear, that everything about you is wrong, etc. etc.

For example, in India among the simpler folk, it is not uncommon for parents to discipline their children in the following ways:

- tie them naked to a tree, so that the passers by, invariably neighbours and known persons, would mock and laugh.

- Throw a mixture of salt/chilly powder into the child's eyes as a punishment.

- Make the child stand near an ant hill where he would without fail be bitten mercilessly.

Their intentions were good. From their very 'ingenious' methods, it is obvious that they themselves were brought up in similar ways and they knew no better. They did what they thought was correct and necessary for the child, not realizing the rejection, shame, fear and guilt that resulted instead. How much healing those same parents would probably need would be an easy guess.

You might recall truths told to you about mum and dad, their backgrounds and relationship, their disputes and quarrels, the difficulties mum had with her in-laws, the complications she had in her pregnancy with you.

Hurts after the age of six

These memories would generally be within our reach and grasp. In addition to the above, which very easily extend into this age as well, for easier identification we could try the following:

Hurts at Home

- Fear of elders, parents and authority.
- Domination, strictness, control of a parent or elder.
- High expectations and perfectionism expected of you. Parents never satisfied with your performance and always pushing you into studies and sports that you do not like.
- Forced to do something against your will.
- Over-attachment and possessiveness of you.
- Quarrels between parents leading to separation and divorce. Apprehension and fear when social workers visited to assess the situation.
- Returning home to an empty house. Having to eat dinner alone, while watching TV.
- Instructions left by way of the answering machine, or notes pasted onto the Frigidaire door. Being sent off to boarding school and summer camps, so that mum and dad could be freer to enjoy their life.

Many such situations and life experiences might be considered standard policy and normal patterns of family life.

One mightn't even consider them to be negative, since everybody is doing it and life in the fast lane demands it.

Perhaps also, over the years families have forgotten how to be family. Their whole idea and concept of family life, living and having fun together, being there for one another, may not quite be what it was in earlier times.

What comes natural to a parent in the East, has to be taught and explained to those of the West. The rough and tumble, lying on his back and twirling the little ones in the air on upraised feet, a gentle pinch or smack on the rump, lying down with the child till it falls asleep etc. are today strange and unnecessary habits for the westerner.

For the easterner, the process of child rearing is a question of nurturing, fostering love and parenthood from the heart. That is why westerners when they visit places in the east, such as India, are struck by their warmth and hospitality.

Possibly to a large extent, for the westerner, *child rearing has become an efficient art minus the tender nurturing love.* Hence easterners visiting the west are struck by their efficiency and politeness; yet coolness in relationships controlled by the weather conditions.

For example, in the West, it is common practice that once baby is put to bed, no amount of crying will draw dad or mum to look in on it. *Advantage:* discipline and good sleeping habits. *Disadvantage:* possible fears, feelings of being alone and rejected, cannot expect dad and mum to be there when needed.

Whereas the eastern tradition still requires mum and dad to nurture and attend to that child. *Advantage:* bonding, security and family values. *Disadvantage:* not as independent perhaps, as the child of the West.

In the West, parents may not correct, discipline and teach their children with a smack on the rump or even a ruler on the flat of their hands. Even when done in love, it is categorized as child abuse and punishable with serious consequences. *Advantage:* the state can keep a tab on actual child abuse and violence and erase it almost totally. *Disadvantage:* Does the child truly learn accountability, respect for elders and gentlemanliness?

Hence give it another thought. Reflect upon your own childhood. How does the above apply and affect you? Would you rather have had it another way? If the possibility of living your childhood again, came your way, what changes would you wish for? Did you miss family and time together? Did you long for mother's gentle touch or dad's rough but secure arm, even though you were a teenager? Or did you reject it because it was the done thing to do?

Hurts at School

- Teachers being partial to other students. Missing your grades because of jealousy and spite.

- peer groups rejecting you, keeping you out of the team and activities, calling you names.

- Taunts, jibes and snubs from older children.

- Vying with others for friendships with the opposite sex. Being used by elders to get what they wanted, for sexual experiments and abuse. Ragging and being put to shame.

- So called friends speaking ill of you and not respecting confidences.

Hurts in College/University/Job

- Disappointments in grades, not being able to choose the stream you wished, being forced against your will to take a different line.

- Relationships with the opposite sex and encounters which have embarrassed you, angered you, left you feeling guilty. Being pressurized into having safe sex and having to take the blame when it was not safe enough.

- Feeling cheated, used, let down by your trusted partner.

- Bearing guilt, financial burden, trauma of ensuing abortion/s.

141

Hurts with Spouse and In-laws

- Spouse more attached to his/her family and friends and permits in-laws to hurt, ill-treat and snub you. This last would be more common perhaps in an Asian home.
- Spouse not accepting you fully, appreciative or encouraging of you.
- Spouse wants his/her own way, abusing you physically and emotionally.
- Spouse having extra-marital affair/s.

Remembering the past may be difficult for some as it very obviously puts you in touch with pain. No one particularly cherishes pain and would thus avoid it where possible. But it would be good to remember that *pain brings about change and change brings about growth.*

Others have developed a spirit of self-preservation to avoid pain and its consequences. They are able to push aside these memories and hurt feelings and carry on with daily routine and work. They become cold and insensitive. Hence beginning this process of recalling, might at first be very technical and without any feelings whatsoever. But as you persevere in this exercise, trying to remember even minute details, you will be rewarded. This exercise will become more realistic and meaningful.

Deaths

Departure of a loved one such as a spouse, a parent, a grandparent, a brother or sister whom you loved dearly and was closely attached to, can be very sensitive and painful, and remain with us a long time. Similarly tragic deaths which you had the misfortune of witnessing, become sources of trauma and even fear.

Often you will have mature adults in their thirties and forties breaking down with wracking sobs, as we touch upon the death of a loved one, which may have taken place a good twenty and more years ago.

There are those who can remember a demised parent only by way of a photograph, as they were too young to recall such an incident. Still others will tell of how a loved one died in a fire, when they were just a babe in arms or a year old. They have obviously learned of this from others as they became old enough to understand.

Initially it would seem there is no hurt or trauma in such memories but as you proceed in counsel and interaction, they are overwhelmed with grief, tears and loss of that parent or loved one. The hurt is beyond the conscious memory and lies in the unconscious.

Crisis Situations

These disturbances invariably cause havoc with our security and lead to fears, confusion and uncertainty.

- Calamities, fires, destruction of house and home
- father losing his job; illness, property disputes with extended family members.
- changing of homes, schools and friends.
- proceedings for separation and divorce

In fact it is not uncommon for children born just around these times to be told by their parents that "When you were born, you brought us bad luck'. One grows up feeling all through life that one really is bad luck. Somehow, wherever you may go, the subconscious makes unhappy things befall you and those whom you touch.

While thinking back on past memories and hurts, the further back you go, the less you might feel is the intensity of hurt. Let this not fool you. You have got to understand that you are now remembering as an adult, maybe even sixty years of age and above. Hurts and memories of long ago especially before the age of six are surely going to be dim and therefore misleading.

But you need to put yourself into the shoes of that little child you once were and relive the negative feelings attached to those memories. For example, remembering a sexual hurt of say thirty years ago is surely not going to be as alive as when it actually happened. Also the effect it had upon you as a child would surely be of a much greater intensity than you might imagine or feel today.

THE UNCONSCIOUS LEVEL

The following exercise will give you great insight into the subconscious and the unconscious part of you. It will help you identify and understand the reason for certain behaviour patterns and attitudes that have always been a question mark to you.

1. Your Position in the Family

Make a little chart as below, of all your brothers and sisters in the family. Mark them in order of ages and chronology, showing clearly the number of years and months between each. Example.

Dad

  .9 B 2.1 G 1.3 G 3.2 G 2.0 B

Mum

B stands for boy and G stands for girl. Above, you have an example of the boys and girls in the family, with the number of years gap between each one. Point 1 or point 2 or point 3 refers to the number of months, i.e., one month, two months, three months. Now let us try to see the possible hurts that each child may have experienced:

The *first* child is a boy and normally, especially in eastern traditions, would be most joyfully welcomed by parents and grandparents. For, to have a son first, is a matter of great pride as the family name is sure to be continued. But this boy is born exactly nine months after mum and dad were married. If they married late and were eager to have a baby soon, then that boy will be much loved. If they married young or at average age then it is quite probable that this boy has experienced rejection.

Under normal conditions and being human, a couple would first want to find their way, get used to one another, settle down into

144

their home; make decisions about finances, jobs, responsibilities, chores, further studies and all it would take to run a home.

However even before they could get down to the nitty-gritty of such matters, they discover that they are soon going to be parents, which was the last thing on their minds. This child has come at the wrong time and smack in the center of their plans. The parents were certainly not quite ready for it. Immediate feelings of the mother such as shock, horror, and an "Oh God, not now!" are sure to impart feelings of being unwanted and a mistake, to the child. Even a fleeting thought to abort at any time, could send messages of fear and rejection into the child.

This kind of hurt though understandable, will nevertheless be the deepest root hurt that will effect the child all through its life, from childhood through marriage. It will be the cause of stubborn behaviour perhaps, anger and rebellion in youth, possible sexual promiscuity, disagreements in marriage, being always demanding, selfish, self-opiniated and so on.

A pattern or history of rejection has been established and will run like a thread all through this person's life. Whenever he gets hurt, it will be in the form of rejection, causing him to react as above. Through this reaction or behaviour he is trying to satisfy the deepest need within him, the need for acceptance and love which he has missed from the time of his conception.

The *second* child has come after experience and is probably wanted, looked forward to and much loved, especially being a girl. As a result, the first child will now begin to feel even more rejection, jealousy and anger as he 'feels', 'thinks', 'sees', daddy and mummy loving his little sister more than him. She is now getting all the attention. In fact he is only one year and four months old when she is conceived.

Soon after, he begins to sense mummy and daddy's attention waning as they begin thinking and concentrating more on the baby to come. He is no longer allowed to stomp and jump happily, on mummy's stomach, as he used to. Soon she cannot carry him and he has to walk behind her. Due to fatigue, which he cannot understand, she cannot spend as much time with him as he would like.

He is only two years of age when sister is born and all the fuss is made of her. Every term of endearment towards his little sister, every cry of hers that gets their attention, emphasizes the 'fact' that he is not loved any longer or at a minimum, as much as she is loved. The root hurt of rejection in the womb interprets all these actions of dad and mum, as 'rejection of himself".

This interpretation is baseless, coming from the subjective feelings of the subconscious and not the objective analysis of the conscious mind. Consequently he will now start behaving in ways to attract and get that attention from dad and mum. He will fuss with his food, mess his trousers, throw anger tantrums, perhaps even hurt little sister and in general behave badly.

Unfortunately, daddy and mummy now begin their own interpretation of his behaviour and instead of loving him and giving him the attention he needs, they will begin the disciplining process of shouting at him, smacking him, punishing him and calling him "a bad boy". He feels the rejection, even more. Rejection takes a deep foot-hold. His whole life is built around it. His foundation is rejection.

The *third* child, might easily experience rejection as she was conceived when her elder sister was only six months old. In all probability daddy and mummy were not quite prepared for her. She has come a little before time and will grow in the shadow of big sister. The *fourth* being a girl will surely feel rejection as Dad and Mum must have by now wanted a second boy. The *last* being a boy will be much loved, pampered, being the youngest and perhaps even spoilt. In some cases he could even become the black sheep of the family.

Sibling rivalry is nothing but each child feeling the other has robbed him or her of mother's lap, love and attention. Hence they grow up always fighting and at loggerheads, never realizing that what they are doing is vying for love. Sometimes they grow out of it but most times they never do. As adults they will never really be close to one another or make special efforts to be in touch.

Perhaps where division of the family property is concerned, they will never agree, thinking the other is benefiting more. The saddest part is that they are so convinced in their mind that their viewpoint, their interpretation, their stand on the matter is correct. Often, those feeling the rejection, will move away from the family, marrying out of their social and financial status, community or even creed.

Child number four will become the Tom Boy of the family because Mum and Dad wanted a boy when she was born. A tom boy is one who behaves and acts as a boy and does all the wild antics a boy would normally do such as climbing trees, jumping over walls, playing rough, etc.

She does so because her subconscious is controlling her behaviour, controlling her to behave as a boy, with the hope that the more she can be that boy, the more she will experience the acceptance and attention of parents, which was missing since conception.

Yet because child number one feels rejected and perhaps does not reach up to parents expectations; and child number five is spoilt and not used to any hard work; she may become the one, mum and dad depend upon most of all. She is the one who gets all the chores and errands done. She is the one who looks after dad and mum in their old age.

Extensions

The above is an example of how the family line can be interpreted. The hurting would change depending on the time placement of each child, whether boy or girl, and the number of children. It should be noted that we are not dealing with stereotypes. Given the same conditions and environment, two children of the same parents might develop, behave, react totally different from each other. Each is unique. No absolute rules or standards can be laid down. Every single person has to be dealt with in an individual and personal capacity.

If for example you are at the tail end of a large family of brothers and sisters, you might hurt deeply from the fact that mother was tired by the time you came on the scene. She just did not have the time and energy to give you.

Or perhaps you are the only boy among a battery of five sisters. You would be so loved and possessed by them all, you found yourself being mothered not by one but by six. For every mouthful of porridge, you had four concerned mothers to feed you. Every time you hurt your little knee, you had five mothers to fuss after you. And to put you to bed, three mummies would sing you a lullaby. And in voices too! Today, though you are an adult, you are an alcoholic or a drug addict because you are desperately attempting to break out of that mothering; you are desperately trying to be independent, free to be your real self.

Others may have additions to their family line up such as death of a child, still-born births, miscarriages, abortions. These too need to be marked clearly on the chart. Such experiences cause guilt feelings, tears of sadness, tension and anxiety whether or not the next child will be born safe and sound. You can be sure that, growing within mother's womb, you have been severely affected by these emotions.

Abortion is considered a grave evil, a grave sin; and experience shows it to have dire consequences upon the persons responsible, the family. Ranging from simple aches and pains that could persist for years, to addictions, rebelliousness of the children, family tensions and break-ups.

Apply Caution

However in analyzing yourself from this little chart, take care not to presume. You are sincerely searching not your known self, but that part of you which is hidden within the subconscious and even the unconscious.

You would need to stay with a fact drawn from the above, let it play in your mind, allowing other known data about your behaviour patterns to surface, make the connections and finally let the conviction settle in. You would need to imagine what mother went through during those situations and circumstances and realize as a consequence, what you too went through.

148

Whatever is analyzed, must have a base, a proof, a connection, an explanation, an extension; into your behaviour patterns, your health, your relationships, your emotional set up. Jumping to conclusions will not serve you in the least. You might find yourself jumping to the wrong ones and futilely working in the wrong direction. Hence this kind of analysis has to be done carefully.

Example 32: Cynthia

I am the eldest child (Daughter) in my family, followed by 3 sisters. Since childhood I was compared with my siblings either look-wise, talent-wise, performance-wise and in every other way. Consciously, I never took it seriously, but I realize it has left its mark on me.

One of which was a lack of Acceptance. This negative feeling of un-acceptance immersed so deep within me that I too could not accept myself as I am. I too began comparing myself with the beauty of other girls around me.

Secondly, whenever anyone expresses care, concern or affection towards me, I suspect and doubt their genuineness.

Thirdly, I would have a tough time during my menses feeling uneasy, uncomfortable and wished God made me a boy for those 3-4 days. I could not go out to work or any outing. I always wanted to stay back at home.

Fourthly, I was shy and timid by nature.

Fifthly, I was a very arrogant person, I could never forgive anyone easily especially outsiders. There were times if I was angry with someone I never spoke for days together.

The root of all these problems was in the fact that Mum and Dad were expecting a boy as their first child, when I was born.

Finally, I was healed of my fear of darkness, of staying alone, of places. This came about as follows:

When I was 6-7 yrs old, my mom was expecting again, and moved to her mothers town. Due to my schooling, I had to stay with a very strict aunt. Unfortunately she too had many family problems to deal with. Since I had afternoon school, she would keep me alone at home, locked inside the house while she went to reach her kids. She lived in an apartment but what scared me most was the emptiness of the home. She would return after an hour. I would be waiting for her all alone, transfixed, never moving from my position.

2. Your Behavioural Patterns

Here we cannot provide absolute or hard and fast rules of behavior, but rather strong indications. The first broad grouping would come under the heading of:

INSECURITIES

Extremely strict and dominating. You must have your own way always, whether at home or at work or at your Church Council. It can only be in this particular manner, leaving no room for discussion, no scope for creativity from others. The children must dress-up in a certain manner, behave in a certain way. They have to be home on the dot of seven. A minute late and they get the treatment. Their time, their friends, their recreation is closely monitored by you. There is no room for freedom and space. Instead of creating an atmosphere of trust and openness, you have created one of regimentation, rebellion and anger, fear and suppression.

Sweeping Statements. You are in the habit of making statements like:

'I am the boss here, you will listen to me' or

'I am the boss because I know what I am doing' or

'God cannot speak through anyone and everyone but only through his appointed leaders, and I am he'.

Your statements and your attitudes indicate that only you

know what you are doing, everyone else is wrong, there is no room for other viewpoints and opinions.

Demanding Bully is what the above makes you. Not necessarily always the case, but probably.

Possible Root Causes

1. Your parents were extremely strict, dominating or harsh with you, that you meteer out the same treatment you received.

2. You were spoilt as a child, you were always given into, you always got your way. You have grown up believing that whatever you demand or expect, you will receive as your right. Hence as an adult at home or office you continue to live the same attitude and belief.

FEELINGS OF INSECURITY

There are those who feel insecure about themselves and within themselves, about the job at work, about running a home, about their profession or the line they have chosen. They are not totally comfortable and at ease where they are.

Lack of Confidence: You lack the confidence required to handle things, to confront others, to face the future, in your ability to perform. You may be intelligent, have great practical skills and innovative ideas; but lack the confidence to put it across to the boss. Superiors and others can sense this weakness and often enough take advantage of the situation.

Indecisiveness. You find it impossible to make decisions by yourself. You consult a million others for their advice. You go back and forth from one opinion to another. You churn it around in your head. Finally with great trepidation you make the decision and take that very hesitant first step. When things do not go well for you, you immediately put the blame onto everyone else, instead of taking the responsibility yourself.

Critical and Judgmental. You have this bad habit of always finding fault with the children and colleagues at work. You put them down, highlight their weak spots, rarely able to see the good in others and build them up with positivity.

Scrupulosity. A feeling of doubt or uncertainty, that the action taken, is correct or just. Often pertains to tiny unimportant details especially in regard to spirituality. Indicates the manner in which the conscience has been trained.

For example: A beggar comes to the door and out of pity you hand him some money. Later you wonder whether you have done a good deed or encouraged him to remain a beggar. It plays upon your mind and robs you of your sleep.

For example: You have confessed your sins to the priest in preparation for Sunday service. Just before the service you have yelled and screamed at your little daughter. You do not feel worthy enough to attend service before confessing again.

You must be perfect in all the small and unimportant details, lest you do wrong, lest you offend others and God. You must check for mistakes at all times. You do not give yourself the freedom to go ahead, until everything is perfect and without blemish. And that time invariably never arrives.

Lack of Order in your life. You work from moment to moment, you jump from one thing to another, without planning and ordering your day. You look for some important papers and you do not know where you have kept them. This could apply to office, to house and home. You end up exhausted because you find yourself running around in circles trying to accomplish your jobs.

Too Many Involvements. You are involved with a hundred different activities, clubs, social programmes; you accept every invitation to get involved, to help, to be of service. You do not know where to draw the line. You end up with burn out. All because you are seeking appreciation, you want to feel important, accepted, appreciated.

Possible Root Causes

1. Strict and dominating upbringing though not as severe as earlier mentioned.

2. Receiving criticism and ridicule from parents, teachers and others in authority.

3. Being compared to others. Lack of appreciation and encouragement.

4. Lack of parents love due to death, separation or paving of careers. Inability of parents to express their love to the child by way of physical touch like hugs and kisses. Parents had no time for the child. Child was brought up by his grandparents or in a crèche.

These root causes can also cause the following:

Poor self image. 'I cannot see anything good at all in myself. I have no gifts, no talents. I look awful, I dress awful. I am ugly, dull and good for nothing. I am a mistake and always will be. I should never have been born.' At an extreme, you come to hate yourself.

Seeking Appreciation and the Limelight. You always wish to be at the microphone speaking your heart out, or on the stage so that all can see you, or a busy-body so you can be noticed and feel important. Your dress weird, wear the craziest of hats, cover your face with earrings, paint your hair different shades of orange and green; so that people will notice.

Failure. Today you are a failure in anything you try your hand at. Nothing seems to work out; not your business, not your spiritual life, not your marriage. Nor can you keep a steady job. This too, even though you are an expert at your work. The above possible root causes will find you your answer but, perhaps especially the fact that as a child you were made to feel a failure, by words and actions, e.g. When a child you were cursed by your parents having broken their favourite vase.

FEELINGS OF REJECTION

Angry and Hot Tempered. You flare up easily, perhaps especially when you are not being taken seriously enough or listened to; when your authority and truthfulness is being questioned, when things are not done the way you would like them done.

Defiant and Rebellious. Your never follow the rules or traditions. You always want to be different. You reject authority and challenge the system.

Shy, Loner, Introvert. You travel into yourself, you become a bookworm, you do not make friends easily, you are satisfied with your own company. Perhaps there is a subconscious fear of being rejected by society, friends and those you are willing to allow yourself to get close to.

Sickliness. You are forever coming down with some illness or the other. One day it is a backache, the other it is a cold, followed by migraine, etc.

Possible Root Causes

1. Parents wanted a boy but you were born a girl and vice versa.
2. You came too soon after marriage or after the previous child.
3. While pregnant with you, mum went through trauma, fear, anxiety, anger through a situation concerning loved ones.

This amounts to unacceptance, unwantedness. The subconscious influences your behavior in such a way so as to get that acceptance and attention, though in a negative way.

Example: by shouting and screaming at everyone, people automatically pay attention; by being adventurous and going a different route or defying the rules and authority, you automatically get the attention of the bosses; by falling sick you get the attention of mother, spouse, nurses and doctors.

Lack of acceptance and love also leads to things like the outrageous: Punk Hairstyles and weird outfits.

Asthma. Asthma often can be a consequence of this kind of hurt. Struggling for breath is likened to the struggle for life, the struggle for acceptance, attention and love.

FEARS

The Dark. You were locked in a room; chased by an animal at night; told stories of ghost and spirits; woke up in the middle of the night to find mummy and daddy were no where to be found; in fun, a pillow was pressed over your face.

Water. An accident when a child, saw you drowning in a pond or struggling to get out of the water.

Height. You fell down a deep hole or worse still, fell off your bunk bed one night.

Animals. You were chased or bitten by a dog when a child. Or perhaps it was a stuffed toy like a hairy lion that momentarily caused you asphyxiation, when a babe in arms.

Authority. Today as an adult you fear your boss and others wielding authority, because those persons in authority are in your subconscious representing your father or that person you grew up to be afraid of.

Losing friends. Perhaps because your closest friends had to leave town, died or for some strange reason broke away from you. On each occasion you were left empty and lost. Or again as it was in the case of Sheila; her most prized possession and the love of her life, her pet rabbit, whom she looked after so dearly every day was found missing. On enquiry, mother told her it was in the pie for supper. In addition she developed a hatred for her mother who took away from her, her best friend.

A Nervous Anxious Fearful Personality. You are the worrying type. You worry over your children, you worry before you leave the house, you imagine all sort of things are happening to your family. Any suggestion for an outing or an adventure and you express your fears before the suggestion has even been properly completed. You experience perspiration and sweating of palms.

Insomnia, Walking/Talking in sleep. Obviously, signs of tension and fear.

Possible Root Causes

Often the roots of the above will be somewhere in the subconscious. However it will not be strange to find them located in your mother's womb.

OTHERS

Physical Illness. As we have seen, many if not most, of our physical ailments would have a root in our emotions. Understanding what negative emotions are at the bottom of our present physical ailment, can lead to healing quickly, easily and surely more economically.

Hunchback. As in the case of Diedre, example no.29 in chapter seven.

Accident Prone. A form of severe insecurity. You need to locate the root which could be any one or more of the roots already mentioned above.

Anorexia. Ashok used to live on a few grapes for each meal. Anorexics are terrified of gaining weight and becoming fat. They feel better about themselves and believe others will accept and respect them more, if thin. But thin is not enough. For some it could be a subconscious willingness and desire to die.

ROOT CAUSE: Deep emotional hurt due to rejection and unacceptance. This could result in a consequent dislike and hatred for self on the one hand; and a compulsion to prove oneself through rebellion, a strong self-will, perfectionism; on the other hand.

Dyslexia. An impairment in the proper use of words while reading, writing and speaking. Children can be described as slow and confused. Experience points to a confusion that exists in the child, of its identity – probably due to one of many factors enumerated thus far. It is the attempt used by the subconscious to acquire that extra attention and clear up the crisis of identity.

156

Adoption. Those who have been adopted, have first been totally rejected and abandoned by their biological parents. Certain character and personality traits can be observed. Adopted persons often have that deep inner need and urge to find out who their real parents were and/or why they were rejected. Their inner spirits can rest only after knowing and understanding.

Healing for this rejection and emptiness is a crucial need. They need to learn and know and feel that they are beautiful and acceptable as they are. The wisdom with which they are brought up by their adoptive parents and family, contribute in this healing process.

Twins. Often feel compelled to compete with one another for attention and acceptance. Sometimes the one born second, grows in the shadow of the first. Different kinds of twins will have different percentage of proximity and closeness to one another. It is imperative to parent them with wisdom such that each develops a healthy identity and self-worth.

Divorce. A divorce shatters the security and confidence of a child. Because divorce is so common today, the effect upon the child is often overlooked. A child is made such, that he/she must have both parents. The inner spirit, the inner life of the child has not been made to handle life with only one parent. The influence of father and mother, both are required to make that child a full human being. The very inner fabric and tissue of the child's spirit is torn to shreds when divorce takes place.

Rape. Needless to explain the effect upon the person, as it is well known by now. Healing is possible through counsel and faith.

Incest involves sexual molestation of a girl, by her father or even brother. Especially when done over a period of time, the effect remains not only upon the emotions but enters the dimension of the spirit as well. The effect is so drastic and traumatic, it can be akin to demonic in nature.

Excessive Bonds. Often a parent can be over-attached, possessive, over-protective of a child. The child consequently does not have the freedom to grow and develop independently and to its full potential. Often addictions to alcohol and other chemicals set in, as a means of breaking away, turning away from such control. The person has the need to break from such a control and bond, in order to find his/her way in life.

It is understood that at marriage, a person is called to leave mother and father and cleave to his spouse. Leaving mother and father is not merely a question of leaving the home he grew up in and finding another place of residence for himself and his spouse. It involves the need to leave emotionally, to cut the emotional umbilical cord, to become a separate entity.

However, every hurt, in some way prevents one from growing free and independent, whole and secure, becoming a separate entity and identity. In some way, every hurt ties us down to parents or someone in one's childhood. Therefore every hurt in some way ties us to that emotional umbilical cord.

Premature Babies. Nature has planned that a baby is required to be nine months in the womb so that it can be shaped and formed to satisfaction. Many babies however are born premature. Some, due to physical conditions of the mother's womb, but most others due to emotional stress and traumas that the mother has faced during her pregnancy. Such babies would certainly need healing for

1. The stress and trauma that the mother experiences which are conveyed to the baby.

2. The baby has to start living, expending energy, exerting itself well before due date as high expectations are now placed on it, to live independently from the mother.

Example 33: Mathew

My wife Christina was due our fourth child, around August 10th. He was born on June 25th. Doctor could not come to a conclusive reason as to why. But we feel he would probably need healing for the following reasons:

1. He was conceived 8 years after our last child. Hence

for a very short time in his life – say a couple of weeks in the womb, he was unexpected and a surprise.

2. Christina was already aware/anxious that as the previous child was born 3 weeks early, this one too had every likelihood of being born before time. Future plans were made accordingly.

3. All our friends wished us a girl as we already had three boys. So sure it was going to be a girl, that gifts and presents were already being planned in pink.

4. While in the womb, he had not to lift a finger or exert a thumb. Everything was done for him. Coming early meant he lost six weeks of coziness, laziness and good food. He had to begin fending for himself; learning to suckle much before his time, exerting that much energy to get food into his little body. He had to be awakened at regular intervals for his feeds. He was not allowed to sleep endlessly like he would have been doing for another six weeks.

5. Infantile jaundice hit him, which meant medication, blood tests and other such hurting and irritating inconveniences.

6. The moment he was born, we hardly had time to look at him, say hi and bless him, when he was whisked away to the NICU (Neo-natal Intensive Care Unit) for necessary warmth and attention. We could look at him for the next 24 hours only through a glass window. He missed being fed at the breast, hearing his mother's heart-beat which he knew by now so well. My wife was first able to hold him and feed him only 24 hours later.

7. For ten days he was in the NICU during which time he was taken care of, by caring but strange hands; he was fed mostly from a bottle as he was too weak to suckle. He was deprived of his mother's touch, nearness, comfort and smell. You can be sure he missed out on his mother's and father's attention and love.

One's immediate reaction to all these points listed might be "what rubbish" "why make such a big fuss over nothing. It happens every day". But this is precisely it. We look at this whole episode and this little baby from an adult mind and thought pattern, using reason and our great intellect. But we need training to look at this situation from the babies point of view. What was he going through and how did he feel at every situation and development.

Can he reason and understand why all this was done to him. Can he understand and accept the reason why he was deprived of his mother's intimacy and attention. Do you honestly think his thought pattern went like this "you know they are taking great care of me. This is the best for me at this moment. I understand therefore why mum is not near me 24 hours of the day. No problem".

In short; apart from the traumas, anxieties and tensions, he would need a healing from very high expectations that were placed upon him. Expectations to do and perform much before his time.

MISCARRIAGES AND ABORTIONS

The death of babies in the womb, at birth, before full term can have the following effects:

1. The babies themselves, if we believe they have a soul, an inner spirit, would still need a healing from fear, rejection, violence.

2. The mother goes through a trauma, an incomparable pain. If in this frame of mind she conceives again, that child in the womb would certainly need healing picked up from its mother in the womb.

Quote from an e-mail

"In the USA, 45 million innocent unborn Americans have lost their lives through abortion since the early seventies. And those lives have been lost in particularly brutal ways. They were torn limb from limb. They were burned. Their skulls were pierced with scissors and their brains were sucked out. And it all took place in the clean, sterile environment of our medical centres. It was legally sanctioned and happened for no other reason than that those lives were inconvenient.

Meanwhile, the Canadian government has allowed the destruction of three million babies in the womb, has allowed scientists to use their vulnerable bodies for human experimentation".

Not counting the millions killed in Europe and the rest of the world the idea here is not to make a political plea but to further the quest of this book, along the thoughts and ideas already mentioned.

In chapter five we have spoken of the outer life and the inner life that every human has. Both begin at conception. We have also recognized that while the outer life provides the physical, the inner life gives rise to the emotional and spiritual. The emotional, spiritual and physical act as one, each one influencing the other, all working together as one.

Using psychological principles that have emerged from the Americas and Europe over the years, we have come to understand that every child within the womb, from the moment of its conception, feels positive and negative. That embryo, that fetus, that unborn child, can feel accepted, loved and cherished; or unwanted, rejected and abandoned.

When wanted, the child feels recognized and important. It develops an identity, a sense of belonging, that it is part of a family and community. It has a role to play in God's plan and in society. Thus, at various levels it is bound in relationship to mother, family, community and society at large.

When aborted, the opposite happens. Firstly as described above, it feels physical torture and pain as its body is broken and cut to pieces. It also experiences the pain of total rejection, murdered by its own parents. It feels the pain of being

161

unrecognized, treated as unimportant, as garbage, a rag doll; with absolute disrespect and no concern whatsoever, for its existence, its rights, its purpose on this earth. And all of this pain is felt in the inner life, i.e., the inner spirit.

After the abortion, the physical remains are discarded, presumably in an ethical manner. But are any steps taken to deal with the inner life, as just described? Though physically dead, the Spirit which God has breathed into it, that is the source of the inner life, remains in turmoil, pain, unrest. Healing is required for the inner spirit, the inner life, the process for which can be seen in chapter fourteen.

A MOMENT TO MEDITATE
THINKING MATURELY

The ball is now in your court. What are you going to do with it?

You have a choice ahead of you.

- Give up
- Ignore it
- Run away
- Face it head on while hoping for victory

Here is where you, dear reader, have to think maturely. Take time off and think for yourself. Let not others do the thinking for you.

Put aside for a moment, the bombardment from the crowds and your peer group, the decibels from your radio and television, the onslaught from the media and the Internet.

Get into a quiet corner somewhere and weigh the pros and the cons. Get in touch with your SQ, i.e., your spiritual quotient.

Let your SQ direct that inner search to seek the higher calling of life, that inner quality to desire truth, meaning and purposes in life. That ability to ask:

- "Who am I"
- "Where is my life heading"
- "Can this be the right path"
- "What response do I make?"

What does your SQ say? What does it prompt you to do?

All that has been written thus far, is based on sound psychological findings and deliberations.

What are you going to let yourself believe? That they are based on truth or that they are a figment of wild imaginations.

Are you hurting from your childhood. Yes or No.

Do you want to be whole?

Or are you going to continue to permit the world and the media to make you their guinea-pig, to dictate to you what direction your life should take?

Are you comfortable with the legacy of obsessions, brokenness, hurt and sexual perversities, that you have been immersed into, that your children have to live with, that you have participated in and left behind for others?

Or do you dare to hope for wholeness and a true peace.

- *A peace that the world and the media cannot provide, no matter how powerful their voice might be, no matter what promises they might make.*

- *A peace that will evade you, no matter how strong your natural inclinations might be, how much pleasure and ecstasy they might provide.*

- *A peace that will remain out of your reach, no matter how strong your philosophical arguments and reasoning might be, no matter the numbers.*

- *A peace that will come your way only through struggle.* The struggle to know the truth and live by it, in a world all around that pressurizes you to believe otherwise. The struggle to understand who you really are and what God's purpose could be for you, here upon this earth.

Chapter Ten

OUR HURTING SEXUALITY

FREUD decided that man was basically and intrinsically sexual or a sexual being. While other more recent psychologists disagree, while there could be other thoughts and ideas upon the subject, there is no doubt that a major part of man is sexual. Sexuality is basic to man, necessary for procreation and intimacy, and controls a major chunk of his life, thoughts and behavior.

In this context what is important to note is that, when a child is hurt emotionally, often enough, mind you often enough and not always, this hurt is transferred to his sexuality and its development and expression. Lack of acceptance and love for example will lead an adolescent to engage in sexual acts with others. Peer groups and free thinking will influence his mind to think it is the 'in thing', the 'mature thing' and that 'there is nothing wrong with it'.

But does that child ever become aware of his deep inner need? A need for a mother and father's love, plain and simple. The subconscious inside him is in control and yearns for the love and acceptance missed. This inner need is transferred now to the sexual in the hope that sex, will meet the emptiness.

FATHER/MOTHER IMAGE

A boy and girl will marry at a very young age, believing they were made for one another and swearing to each other love and fidelity. Invariably, they are not mentally capable of understanding their decision and the responsibilities that go with it. Neither are they emotionally capable of handling the relationship. No wonder then that they break up very soon.

What brings them together at such a young age, often enough even before they have completed their studies, is their individual needs for acceptance and love. No doubt this has become a social trend in the west.

A classical situation would be a man who chooses a woman many years older than himself and vice versa? Invariably this would be because he is looking for a mother figure in the woman, a mother's love he has missed all his life. The same would apply to the woman marrying someone years older than herself, looking for a father image. However, this need is also prevalent often enough in average, normal couples and is one of the most important reasons for couples breaking up a few months or years after marriage.

Each one makes demands upon the other, over and above what one would normally make in marriage. Consciously one likes to believe it may be a convenient arrangement providing financial and temporal security. Subconsciously each one is simply seeking for that love of mother or father missed out in and since early childhood.

How then would this affect the number of children who grow up in a broken home, with a single parent, in a foster home or a home for the abandoned? The following example is an indication.

Example 34: Hyacinth

Distraught with grief, Hyacinth, a sixty five year old grandmother, began confessing to me her guilt feelings of earlier years. The fact that she had been unfaithful to her husband. Something she could not forgive herself for, leave alone understand. "Why," I asked, "has he dealt with you shabbily"? "No, no" she answered, "on the contrary he has been a most loving husband to me".

"Strange" I said, "has he died, has he hurt you in some way, has he not provided for you properly"? "No, no" she said again, "you do not understand. There could not have been a finer man. He has treated me like his queen. He has loved me totally and provided for me and the children, exquisitely."

"What then is your problem" I asked, now rather foxed and unaware where this counsel was leading. "This is why I have come to you. I do not know. I cannot understand myself". Then as if by inspiration I asked, "Why did you have these extra-marital affairs? What did you get out of them? What did you expect or hope to get from these other men"?

After some thought she replied "I think I just wanted them to look after me, to protect me, to be good to me". Something inside my brain clicked and the next question hit the nail on the head as I asked "When did your father die"? "When I was three", she answered.

Though Hyacinth had had a wonderful spouse and family, her inner spirit still yearned and longed for a father, whom she had missed out on, from the age of three. All her life, despite being surrounded by mature love, the child within her kept popping up, looking for that father image.

The need was so strong, she found it in men who in some way were paternalistic towards her. Her conscious mind knew she was treading danger, eventually doing wrong and falling into "sin", but her subconscious feeling the need so drastically and being much stronger than the conscious, took control.

All her life she was plagued with guilt. At the confessional she was given spiritual platitudes and told not to think only of herself. Nothing seemed to help as the idea grew upon her that she was a 'wicked woman'. Understanding her situation, was like rolling a stone off her chest. After prayer, she went away rejoicing and contented.

IRRECONCILABLE DIFFERENCES

Quarrels and bickering in a marriage, put down to 'irreconcilable differences' could be explained in the light of each one's childhood hurts, that have resulted in attitude and behavioral formations. These are merely outward expressions, of an inner need for acceptance, understanding, justice and love.

One needs to be dominating, the other quiet and submissive. One is hyperactive, never able to sit and relax, the other waiting for quiet evenings to spend together. One is a workaholic, the other left to do the dishes and wait endlessly for supper. One loves executive parties, the outdoors etc. while the other wants more of God in the family. The story goes on endlessly....

They reach a state of incompleteness, loneliness, unhappiness; two individual minds and hearts beating separately and moving in opposite directions. The resulting unfaithfulness and adultery, is not so much a question of losing interest in the other or 'falling-out' of love. Rather it is the endless search to fill their basic needs as child, boy or girl.

And finally what about couples married for many years having attained the distinction of being parents and even grandparents. Why on earth would they want to break up and go through the right awful mess of divorce and resulting separation of assets and wealth? Could it be that as long as children are with them, their minds and hearts are occupied. But once the birds have flown the coop, what is left of their minds, their hearts, their bodies, is not sufficient to complete the other. The emptiness of their childhood, that little boy or girl they once were, now cries out to be met.

'The eternal foundation' in chapter 5, sheds more light on the point.

BOY/GIRL ISSUES

It is an understandable human desire for parents to want a boy or a girl when planning a home. When a boy is hoped for, planned for and even prayed for, the girl that emerges, feels the wrath of rejection. In what way can that girl be affected. How is her character and personality going to take shape?

The subconscious controlling 90 per cent of that child's mind, invariably directs her to behave as much as possible as a boy. The more she can behave, be and act that boy, the more will she receive that acceptance and love from parents. This is the basic idea and is seen in the following:

1. *Becoming a tom-boy:* By dressing up as much as a boy, participating in sports and activities generally reserved for the boys, and becoming the handyman around the house for dad and mum.

2. *Physical Development:* Often and perhaps in quite extreme cases, the physical growth of this girl will be curtailed. Breasts and sexual organs are also stunted in their development.

3. *Menstrual Cycles:* It is not surprising therefore that at adolescence, during her teens and through her whole life, she would face difficulties as under:

   • Irregular periods, with little or no flow at all.

   • Extreme and sometimes excruciating pain at menstruation

Boys have to be boys. Rough and tough is their nature. Boys do not have periods. The subconscious over the years fills her mind with the one big lie – you must be a boy in order to be accepted and loved. The subconscious literally controls the bodily functions of that girl. The subconscious does not use reason or logic or intellect, but the ever strong feelings and desires of the inner person, the inner man, the hidden self.

The subconscious in its attempt to grab and manipulate acceptance and love, takes control and forces that girl to be and behave like boys do. That girl from her conscious mind is totally unaware of her behavior pattern. She knows she is a girl but likes to be different.

Invariably, concerned mothers feed their daughters on medication in order to regularize their menstrual cycles. Extreme pain and discomfort results in humiliation and necessitates staying away from school/work/outings.

4. *Childlessness.* Furthermore, boys do not have babies. Applying the same principle, the subconscious, believing that girl is or needs to be a boy, even prevents conception. To overcome her pain at barrenness, all sorts of medication and sexual techniques are attempted. The disappointments and

frustration they go through is pitiable, thus necessitating the whole rigmarol and process of adoption.

However there could be other reasons why a woman finds herself unable to conceive.

Example 35. Janice

Janice had tried for years, to conceive a child. She longed for a child. She yearned to be a mother. All the advice given her by sex therapists and the use of techniques for penetration, failed. Hers was not a question of rejection. Hers was even more subtle.

Her only brother had been the pampered one. He grew up believing he was the centre of attraction and everything had to revolve around him and his life. In his adulthood he became a waster, a troublemaker. He brought shame to the family while running amuck. He was the black sheep of the family.

When Janice married, though she was eager to have a family of her own, she abhorred boys lest they might turn out like her brother. Boys in her mind gave far too much trouble, inflicted pain and humiliation to the nearest and dearest, and were sure to ruin the peace in the family. Her subconscious was influenced by years of negativity towards her brother, resulting in a positive dislike and distrust of boys. With the possibility that the children she bore could well be boys, her subconscious decided not to conceive any at all.

5. *Marriage:* And what about women who never seem to find the right guy to settle down with, in marriage? In the Indian tradition, though quaint but still prevalent, parents have to look for compatible suitors for their daughters. Sometimes they are willing to travel to 'hell and back' and often go berserk, trying to get their daughters to say 'Yes'.

After scores of 'teas' and prayer Novenas, they throw in the towel, grumpy at their daughter's stubbornness and the resulting insult to the family. Despite the many attempts, nothing seems to work out. The daughter is labeled as hard-nosed, rebellious, disobedient. But how many care to understand what those 'poor daughters' go through.

Example 36: Sujata

Sujata is Christian. Her parents grew frustrated that she could not decide on any of the many suitors they had presented to her. In desperation, they took the advice of well-meaning Hindu neigbours, who organized a puja (a kind of prayer service to the gods) for this purpose. A Hindu pujari (like a priest) was called to the house and performed a ritual of killing a cock bird in the home and saying some mantras (prayers).

Unfortunately nothing happened for poor Sujata. From then on, every year a different pujari was engaged, each supposedly more powerful than the previous one. But at the end of five years, Sujata was still single with no silver lining to be seen.

Having attended our programme, we learned that, at the time when Sujata was conceived and born, her parents had wanted a boy. Her subconscious therefore used its full capacity and power to make her behave and be that boy, for reasons explained already. Ninety percent of her being, leaned towards being that boy.

However, from her conscious mind she was definitely a girl. Facts and figure proved it! She very much wanted to marry, which would also please her parents. Consciously she had no desire to be rebellious, or disobedient or difficult. But her conscious state comprised only ten percent of her whole being.

When suitors were brought to her, a tug of war took place between her conscious mind that wanted to be normal and marry, and her subconscious that said "I am a boy and therefore cannot marry a boy". Her subconscious rebelled at the idea. Boys do not marry boys, or anyway that is the tradition!

On the other hand, being effeminate, developing inadequately physically, being responsible for childlessness in marriage, can also hold true for the boy whose parents wanted a girl at his conception and birth. The subconscious is simply doing the opposite in this case, i.e., attempting to turn that boy into a girl such that 'she' will get the attention and acceptance and love from the parents.

Taking this whole topic further, we might understand the need that many have, to change their gender by artificial means. Compassionate as one might be for such persons, who are obviously deeply unhappy with themselves, a deeper study needs to be made from the emotional, the spiritual as well as the family tree, angle. Healing in one or more of these areas will bring the self-acceptance and peace of mind, sorely needed.

SEXUAL ABUSE

A woman sexually abused as a child could turn out to be a man-hater; marriage becomes repulsive, the sexual act with her husband becomes filthy and degrading. The very touch of a man be it friend or foe brings with it feelings of fear and anger.

Repeated exposure to sexual abuse as a child could make one vulnerable to the sweet talk, gentle words and caring concerns of men, who in their deceit only use her to meet their sexual needs. Or a deep hatred for self could set in, a hatred for one's own gender and body.

HOMOSEXUALITY

On the one hand there is a growing number of people; professionals, the medical profession, politicians, psychologists and others who vehemently postulate the theory and belief that homosexuality is passed on in the genes and therefore you can do nothing about it but accept it and nourish it, taking the attitude of "that's the way I am".

On the other hand there are many more; also professionals, the medical profession, politicians, psychologists, Church groups and others who oppose this idea from its inception, pointing out a number of inconsistencies and flaws with this stance. They are of the opinion that the proponents of this idea, in their eagerness to prove a point; in their rush to justify their own personal beliefs and relationships, in their dire need to put at ease, uneasy consciences; have hastily jumped to conclusions. The veracity of their claims and the evidence collected from medical study and research is insufficient and inconclusive.

The media has contributed a major share in this battle of the sexes. They have misused and even abused the sanctity of the written and spoken word; flouted their power and authority to cater to the masses, thereby hugely succeeding in selling their product. Therefore they say, propagating such an idea speaks of immaturity, irresponsibility, large scale distortion of the facts; misleading innocent masses and particularly the youth.

Much printed information is freely available for and against. The internet offers even more and it would be futile to repeat any of this here. Yet in order to put this whole controversy into proper perspective *we must first look at some very basic, very obvious, very fundamental truths, which have been grossly overlooked in an eagerness to push one's own agenda. We look at the bare necessities, the simple facts of life.*

1. Male Female Phenomenon

The phenomenon of male and female permeates every aspect of life and creation. It applies to the birds of the air, the fish in the sea, animals and insects, plant and marine life, as well as the inimitable human being. Without the two co-existing from the beginning of creation, nature and man would never have been able to sustain themselves. They would have died out at the very first generation itself. Male and female have always been established as two, but to operate as one; to reproduce, to regenerate, to sustain and continue that wonderful work of 'creation'. Without the principle of male and female, this could never have happened all these millions of years.

In fact, this has become for creation and all life that exists, a basic philosophy and thought pattern, a motivation and culture to further and continue life and all its species. The thought pattern is so deeply rooted that even in the sciences such as electricity, the principle of male and female holds fast in order to generate, use and transfer electric current.

Be that as it may, mythical or fundamentally true, to save and continue all of God's creation, two by two, *male* and *female*, did Noah ticket all God's creatures into the "ARK". And though it has been only more recently that medical science could 'germinate' an embryo, nevertheless without male and female, without a woman's womb, the process cannot be completed.

2. The Sexual Organs

(i) The sexual organ of man, the erect penis, is made such so as to fit neatly, comfortably and perfectly into that of the woman's, i.e., the vagina. No other part of the woman's body (leave alone another man's body) is sculpted to receive the penis with the same effectiveness and result. It would seem logical and sensible that as with nature, the male sexual organ finds compatibility and purpose, only with the female sexual organ and not with any other part of her body or that of another man.

No doubt, in order to gratify their needs, oral and anal sex have become a substitute for homosexual men. However, the consequent tearing of tissues and linings; infections, disease and even AIDS, is well known and documented. For the lesbian women, no penetration of any kind is possible without an external gadget. Could therefore these and other such expressions of sexuality be natural or normal between humans? Do they lend to peace, comfort and dignity between the parties? Finally could this in any way be a sign, a symbol of that 'higher calling' of man?

(ii) The sexual act enjoyed in this way, results in the highest form of excitement and pleasure to the man and woman separately, and as a result to both. Each one's excitement fuels the other. Doing it with any other orifice in the body or with a person of the same sex cannot provide the compatibility, the same intensity of pleasure to each one and as a result to both. For the simple reason that, besides other erotic zones, only and only the vagina in the woman's body is sculpted to respond when evoked, affirmed, caressed and penetrated by the male penis, to provide that level of excitement and pleasure, sense of contentment, fulfillment and unity.

(iii) To make that sexual act complete, there is first the thrusting, the giving, the emptying from the part of the man. *That is his nature and quality.* This giving, this emptying, needs to be met with a reciprocal action; needs to be received and accepted, resulting in a filling-up-with. This can only be accomplished through an attitude of yielding, from the part of the woman. *This is the quality and nature of woman*; to yield, to submit, to take in. This 'completeness', this 'compatibility', can never be achieved between two persons of the same sex.

(iv) In his eagerness to thrust and finally ejaculate millions of sperm in his semen, no other part of the woman's body (this time you can forget the man totally) is sculpted to receive it and knows what to do with it. Only the vagina is structured such and knows what to do with it. The woman's vagina alone can receive the semen with eager longing, can even allow it to fertilize her own egg and have it travel to the womb where it is allowed to grow into a little human baby.

This seems to leave little doubt if any at all then, that the sexual organs of man and woman were made for each other. There can be no doubt that they make a perfect match, a perfect fit. They complement one other. They were created for each other; to provide sexual pleasure, for reproduction and to aid that man and woman grow into unity.

3. Nature as Against Man

The discovery of homosexual type of behaviour in nature such as penguins, sheep, rats, gulls etc. is used as a strong leverage to prove homosexuality among human beings. Apart from arguments for and against the same; apart from the flaws and discrepancies pointed out in the mode and manner of research conducted; those proposing these theories, discoveries and conclusions, forget one simple truth. *Man is not an animal.*

Man has that inner life of the spiritual and the emotional, which is incomparable with any other living creature upon this earth. This makes him unique and distinct from the animal world and the rest of nature. This inner life provides him identity and character, a quality and purpose to life, far above that of the animal kingdom. Refer again to chapter V.

One great characteristic of this inner life is, the ability, the desire, the need to love and to be loved. In this ability, desire and need; he expresses feelings from the innermost heart; of tenderness, caring, surrender, trust and unity. All of these can and is expressed through his sexuality. His sexuality is an aid and a help to express his love and to draw closer in unity. His sexuality is subordinated to his loving nature.

But Man's ability to love is not limited only to and through sex. His loving on a wider level goes beyond sex and into the dimension of the family, community and the spiritual. Sex is only a small part of his total call to love.

Not so with animals for which sexuality and much of their behaviour is pure instinct. To even begin to compare sex in nature with that in man, *speaks of his folly and low self-esteem.* Man is certainly much superior to animals and creatures. He has over the years learned to take control and authority through his intelligence. He has learned to subdue all creatures to his authority and power. He it is that rules Governments and Nations, Space and the Oceans. Not the animals of the earth.

Why is it then, that in the area of sex and sexuality, all distinctions have been put aside? Poor man is now removed from his pedestal of honour, is stripped of his intelligence and power, and is now made equal to that of animals and creatures. Why is it that sexuality in man, his orientations, his likes and dislikes is organized, understood and even determined by animals and nature?

176

The only answer could be "it is most convenient in this day and age". To change things, to restore man to his full glory, to heal the brokenness in man, is too difficult a task.

4. Sex as against Love

What is the whole purpose of sex? To make out? To produce excitement, pleasure, enjoyment, ecstasy? Or a means to develop a relationship, growth into intimacy, trust, surrender, love?

The world of film stars, singing sensations, sports legends and other entertainment masters have successfully separated sex from love, placing it high on a pedestal to be worshipped.

You cannot become popular or successful without exhibiting a strong sexual sleazy tone; through lyrics, stage antics, displaying a complete assortment of assets for the media, making and breaking relationships in rapid succession, granting sexual favours, suing the media, suing one another, robbing one another's partners, husbands or wives.

The pressure upon them is high. The demands made even greater. This results in tragic deaths such as in the case of Marilyn Monroe and Elvis Presley. Elvis once said: *The image is one thing and the human being is another...it's very hard to live up to an image.*

If allowed to retreat into the quiet of their inner self, especially the new and upcoming stars; it would be interesting to know how many detest the image being portrayed of themselves and seek the first opportunity to change it.

Sex has superseded love. Good sex is the all-important objective. Articles and interviews with the media, questions put to "Sex Experts" are all about having 'good, healthy and safe sex'. 'How to synchronize orgasm with...', 'how to make your man happy in bed', 'should you do it with your ex', 'can vaginal be replaced by anal ....' 'how pre-marital and masturbation can increase your joy with your spouse..' and worse.

Love and relationships are secondary. Sex has been alienated from its context. Its primary role and purpose, .ie., to

177

encourage and deepen a committed love relationship, has been eliminated, has been side-tracked. Sex in itself, has become the greater value, the greater goal. No wonder then that in determining sexual orientation of men and women, in attempting to prove a point, the focus narrows down to sex and its expressions minus the context within which it is placed.

Flowing from this thought pattern it is not surprising that sexuality in man is contrasted with, weighed against, determined by, sexuality in nature and animals, the other resident creatures upon this earth. To do so, man has to be reduced to the same level as penguins, gulls, sheep and even rats!

How awful! Degrading? A lie neatly packaged.

5. Genes as against Environment

The proponents of homosexuality insist that their orientation is in the genes. While the traditionalists insist that conclusive proof has not been established; it is crucial to understand that the very purpose, function and behaviour of genes and the genetic structure, is to reproduce another. Therefore to state that homosexuality is rooted in the genes, opposes the fundamental purpose and nature of genetic behaviour. It goes contrary to and defeats the very reason the genes structure exists.

It only serves to prove that if such a gene does exist, it could not exist as a result of reproduction. It exists purely because of the environment, and in the context of this book, due to deep hurting experiences and choice behaviour patterns.

However what is also important to note is, researchers defending the gene theory have admitted, that the more a person is subjected to an environment that supports or end results in homosexuality, the more the person engages in homosexual acts; the more likely will the gene if it exists as above, be developed.

Quotes:

Apart from volumes of documented research done, the

mention of one by Dean Hamer would be commendable: *"We knew that genes were only part of the answer. We assumed the environment also played a role in sexual orientation, as it does in most, if not all behaviours...* (Hamer and Copeland, 1994, p. 82)

6. Barely 1 per cent of genetic material mapped

Finally, what is also imperative to realize is that genes themselves constitute barely 1 per cent of all genetic material. In the year 2000 the mapping of the first genome took care of barely 1.2 per cent of all genetic material. The balance 98.8 per cent and its effect was left largely unexplored. The structure of the DNA no doubt is a very complicated issue.

But what follows is a very simple question.

How can anyone - politicians, church groups, professionals, the media, leave alone the medical profession; push for the genetic theory of homosexuality with only 1 per cent of material and factual data? Does this not constitute deception in magnified proportions?

The above arguments might look dispensable in its simplicity. One might be tempted to discard it, it being no new teaching, no new discovery, no complicated philosophy of life. And yet is it not in the simplicity of life that we discover the truth?

If one persists in challenging sociological and psychological principles that have been determined after years of study and research; if one persists in revolting against standard norms of marriage and parenting; if one continually chooses to pamper carnal cravings; and finally if one persists in eliminating God and taking his place; then one has desperately to search for explanations, justifications, meaning and purpose to the human life.

But for those who are truly open to and seeking the truth; for those willing to allow objective reasoning rather than subjective forces to influence them; finally for those willing to understand man's sexuality in context of God's plan and purpose; light will dawn upon their confused and darkened minds causing them to see the effect of the environment and the hurting emotions, upon the sexuality of young men and women growing up into adulthood.

How then does the environment and hurting emotions lead to homosexual orientation and behaviour among young men and woman?

Perhaps more than paedophilia and perverse sexual acts, homosexuality would be a little more difficult to understand. A typical homosexual couple would enact the roles of a man and a woman. One partner takes on the role of the stronger and definitely masculine personality, while the other the effeminate delicate woman, walking, talking and sometimes even dressing as one.

The one taking the masculine role. He wants to be the man. His idea of a man is to be the dominant one, the one on top. His urge is to thrust and ejaculate into the other. But the other must not be a woman, but a woman-like man. Why? He wants to perform the same as any other man in a heterosexual relationship, but not with a woman.

Does he hate women. Is he afraid of them. Has he had a bad relationship of some kind with another woman such as his mother. Was she too dominating and harsh or over-possessive and attached. Such that he cannot relate freely with women, he is not comfortable or trusting of them? In fact, in order to live freely and happily, he needs to break free of the woman who has been binding him all his life. Or has he been greatly deprived of a mother's love?

But being a normal heterosexual would mean dependence upon and need to trust woman, to be able to relate freely, which he cannot do. Thus the only way to live a free and happy life would mean to live with and relate to that woman-like man, a man who behaves like a woman, the woman he has missed, a man who will satisfy also his sexual needs.

. Or again it could be that he has been so emotionally battered by his father and/or others, that he does not feel man enough, to do it with women. He lacks confidence and self-worth.

The one taking the feminine role. He is naturally a man but does not feel like one. He feels more comfortable in the role of a woman, relating as one, delicate and effeminate. In his sexuality he is more comfortable yielding to the other, receiving from the other. Why?

He seems to miss out on the masculinity, which ought to have been imparted to him from a strong and confident father. This could be due to three reasons:

1. His father was a weakling, indecisive, subdued and submissive to his wife. His father could not give him that strong masculine presence that every child needs, in order to experience security and confidence in self. As a result he too grew up lacking enough of the male masculinity and presence in his life to make him a complete person. The feminine from his mother perhaps, was more pronounced and the stronger influence. Thus the need to behave as one.

2. His father on the other hand was overbearing , harshly critical, dogmatic, dominating, regimental in his training. His negative influence upon the son was so strong that it suppressed his true self, suppressed his feelings. He ended up feeling incomplete, useless, a good-for-nothing. His self-image was shattered. Thus he could not stand up and behave as a man ought to. The only aspect that stood up was his feminine side thus causing him to take the feminine role in the relationship.

3. Or again, it is possible that when he was conceived in his mother's womb, his mother/father very much wanted a girl. He experienced rejection, unacceptance and lack of love. Growing up, he became effeminate and girlish in all he did. In his subconscious he is trying to be that girl they wanted, in order to win that acceptance and love he missed out on.

Perhaps others at school tease, make fun and ostracize him. Gradually his mind begins to believe he is and wants to be that girl. And now as an adult and wanting to live out his sexuality, his subconscious dictates to him. He is trying to be a girl, he needs to be that girl, in order to continuously experience acceptance and love from his parents.

Nevertheless, the above factors invariably are supported and encouraged by still other factors and alone are not enough to turn a person into a homosexual. Added to these underlying effects and hurts is the homosexual influence he has been exposed to by others, experimentation and literature.

Exposure. Lack of sufficient and positive love from parents leave a void in his spirit. This void is needing to be filled – with love. A mother's love and/or a father's love. This need is deep, a thirsty longing to be satiated. The subconscious does not use reason to decide what kind of love or sexuality is good, healthy and fulfilling. Exposure to perverse sexual ideas, pictures, experimentation and such like will find a nesting place in the subconscious. Exposure to sexual acts with the same sex will have an even more powerful impact. That girl or boy, now man or woman, without realizing it, is continually on the look out for a mother image or a father image.

The subconscious, having a taste for the same, will begin to take a liking for it and tune in to it. Gradually the subconscious will demand more and more. This is now misinterpreted as "This is the way I am". "These are my normal human feelings, likes and dislikes". "If this is the way I am, if this is the way God has made me, what could be wrong with that?" Here then follows the *decision,* the *choice* that each one makes.

Possibly this could be one of the major reasons why homosexuality is more pronounced in the West, in more permissive societies and cultures, where exposure is at its peak.

If however, he was exposed as above, only to heterosexuality, his subconscious would tune in, realize the need within is being satisfied, and demand more.

182

The possibilities are endless. The combination of factors sometimes make it more difficult/complicated to get to the bottom of things. In analyzing each case what is important is to understand how that particular person has been affected with the information at hand, how his or her psyche has been influenced and 'programmed'. Given the same set of circumstances two people will be affected, each one differently from the other.

Families in the United States of America

Looking at the state of marriages and families in the U.S.A. alone, what stands out as a sore thumb is the fact that, at any given time, 50 per cent and more of marriages have broken-up. Would not this fact by itself, warp the development and growth of 50 per cent of all children in the U.S.A. alone? Sadly American children have got used to the idea of growing up without a secure home, with a single parent or even with a step-parent. Applying the simple rules of psychology, is it surprising then that many children from such broken homes might be affected as below?

Firstly, the parent they are entrusted to live with after the legal divorce and separation, i.e., usually the Mother, is no longer able to be a full-fledged mother to that child. She herself is invariably broken and licking her wounds after a painful battle. She also has to fend for herself financially, emotionally and mentally. Getting into another relationship is almost certainly the next step. The child becomes a second, a runner-up = rejection.

Secondly, even if loving and caring (which often enough is never the case), no step-mother or father could ever replace mum or dad. Missing out on the presence, security and love of any one of the parents would scar them with a life long need and search for a mother image or a father image as the case would be. As a result they do not grow and develop as whole human beings. They begin life with a handicap.

Thirdly, it is no surprise therefore that now adults, many of these children from these broken homes are not able to relate in full maturity with the opposite sex. Their deeper inner need as analysed above, emanating from the subconscious would control their thought and action and orientation. Their natural inclinations often would make them feel more comfortable with the same sex.

Fourthly, their conviction reverberates

• that is me.

• that is the way I feel.

• what could be wrong about my natural inclinations.

In other words what was/is natural and a common factor to most if not to all, due to the environment is now not a common factor. What is unnatural, what is not whole, what is hurting; is now becoming common and demands acceptability.

Finally, the cry even of the homosexual heart is to father and/ or mother a child, a family. That is the deepest desire of every human, man or woman. That is their higher calling, their dignity, their true identity and pride. That is the way the all powerful Creator has made man.

But due to their orientations they refuse to have anything to do with the opposite sex. They are unable to do it with the opposite sex. Due to their orientations they insist on keeping the opposite sex out. Due to their orientations they even hate the opposite sex.

Yet to create family they realize they are unable to develop their seed by itself into a human child. They realize they cannot accomplish it with their partner of the same sex. They realize they just cannot germinate their seed in the earth like any plant. They realize they cannot do without the opposite sex to germinate their egg or sperm.

And thus comes science somewhat to their rescue, through artificial insemination, through surrogate mothers, through the test tube. This time however, minus the excitement, minus the heights of sexual ecstasy, minus the wonder of conception, minus the longing of giving, the beauty of commitment, the joy of love. Minus any contact with the opposite sex.

Cool. Every need taken care of. Simple. Easy. Convenient.

A man attempts to love that child as a mother would. A woman attempts to love that child as a father would.

To the common average mind, such parenting is an impossibility and does not make any sense. However living under the deception that he or she can replace the mother or father in that home, little do they take the trouble to understand the effect upon the child that is developed in such manner. Little do they accept the principles and truth that psychology has researched over the years. Little are they open to understanding the emotional and spiritual effects upon such a child. Little are they concerned about these deeper truths, as long as they can have a "family" to call their own.

The law of God would require them to accept their error and change their lifestyles, their orientations, their motivations. However pride and selfishness gets the better of them and they remain hardened knowing that the law and science is behind them.

The all pervading SELF takes precedence. My needs, my desires, my convenience, my orientation is the only thing that counts. I am god.

Once again, so simple, so obvious and therefore not acceptable to human wisdom that is blinded by the needs of the SELF.

OBSESSIONS AND BONDAGES

Example 37: Pierce

Pierce is a grown man some fifty plus years of age. His obsession is with little girls. He likes to touch their private parts and even kiss them. He had got in to trouble many a time and been jailed for child molestation. Sad to say that, whatever attempt he has made to change, he cannot give it up. It seems to have got a hold on him and taken control.

As a child he was bereft of parental love. Introduced to sex by teenage girls they would fondle him and make him fondle them and lick their pubic hair and genitals. This happened over the years. As he matured sexually, his subconscious learned that this was a way to satisfy himself, this was the way to pacify his deep hunger and thirst for parental love he had missed out on.

With Pierce, this was the subconscious way of believing and feeling that, the vacuum of love caused by the lack of parental attention could be filled in this way. It took a hold upon him. The more he was exposed to this kind of sexuality, the more it increased that hold upon him. It became an obsession. It became a bondage.

Now it was no longer merely an emotional weakness stemming from his deep void. But choosing to indulge in this kind of 'wrong', in this kind of 'sin' and abuse of little ones, took him to the level of the spiritual, exposed him to a power beyond simple psychology; trapped or bound him to the forces of evil. The Spirit within him, the innermost circle as shown in figure in chapter five, has now become tainted.

An Obsession or Bondage is something that takes a hold of you. It is a power too strong for you to handle. Your 'Free Will' is not as free as you might think it to be. It is a power that grabs you from within. Your body cannot do without it. Your inner spirit yearns for more and more. Your mind imagines and discovers new ways, new techniques, to make the experience more lasting, more satisfying.

A healing is required. A change is needed for the person to be restored to normalcy and live the full life. Healing can take place through deep counseling, strengthened by prayer and a desire to change, to correct one's ways, to be freed from this situation.

And yet the person is taught to believe that, this mode of behaviour comes 'natural' to him. This is the way he has been created, this is the way he is. It flows easily and without struggle. It gives him a sense of satisfaction. Therefore accepting it, is the most natural thing in the world. Fighting for recognition socially, legally and politically, is the next step.

This is the lie he begins to believe. This is the deception he begins to live in.

Example: **A *practising homosexual.*** He practises what comes natural to him, what seems to flow from within himself. He likes it. It is exciting and pleasurable. He has companionship. He does not see it as an obsession or a bondage. He therefore does not see it as sin, as an evil.

The fact that he has millions of others like him the world over, supports his stand. The fact that the media has systematically lied to the world, claiming that homosexuality is in the genes, encourages him no end. If it is in the genes, you can do nothing about it but accept it.

This is the lie he begins to believe. This is the deception he begins to live in.

On the other hand, is he willing to accept the truth? Is he willing to accept that no medical journal, no scientist, no one and nothing in the medical profession has ever categorically claimed and proven that homosexuality is in the genes? Is he therefore willing to accept that he was never made to be that way but it is the hurts of his childhood that have a vice-like grip over him?

Example: **A *young man afflicted with Masturbation.*** He felt guilty and upset that no matter how much he tried and how fervently he prayed, he could not get rid of this affliction or bondage. On analysis it was discovered that, when a little lad of four, he would be left with the maid at home, while parents were away at work and siblings in school. The maid would abuse him physically and sexually, getting him to paw her and the usual.

Was he guilty of committing any wrong-doing or sin, with the maid? Surely not. He was an innocent lad, ignorant of the ways of the wicked, in the wrong place at the wrong time. He was a victim of circumstances. Yet, the wrong or weakness of that housemaid, left its mark and impact upon him. Her frailty and sin exposed him to an evil, which affected him till date. Today, this hurt of yesteryears, lead him into an obsession, a bondage with masturbation.

One might ask "how come a little child who is innocent, can be influenced by someone else's sin and wrong doing?" This is the mystery of life. If you disturb a thief attempting to burgle your home in the middle of the night and he whacks you on the head, leaving a broken skull and brain damage for the rest of your life, would you still like to ask how his sin can affect you?

Some schools of psychology might insist that what comes to him is the most natural thing in the world and why should he try to change it.

This is the lie he begins to believe. This is the deception he begins to live in.

The house maid obviously had a background of hurt and rejection. It was her way of thirsting for 'Love' which she missed out on, when a child. But her actions left an indelible mark upon that young lad. His healing came about in the following manner:

firstly, through an awareness of the root cause
secondly, correcting the wrong he was doing (today)
thirdly, forgiving the housemaid deeply of all she had done to him.

Example: ***The infamous Josef Fritzl of Austria*** – Wikipedia. Fritzl pleaded guilty to rape, incest, sequestration and grievous assault against his daughter. While the prosecutor accused him of showing no sign of regret or any consciousness of wrongdoing; he put the blame upon his troubled past.

Interesting to note is that in putting the blame upon his past, his childhood; he abdicated responsibility through his own actions and decisions. He excused himself from any wrong, any evil, any sin.

Example: ***Recent happenings discovered in France.*** Where babies and children were sexually abused by their parents and grand-parents, in a sickeningly casual manner. On some occasions, loaned out to others for as little as a pack of cigarettes, a plateful of food, a drink or even as a favour. The law has most certainly convicted a number of persons.

Using the same argument as above, if paedophilia comes

'natural' to someone, why should he be deprived of expressing himself? If that is the way a person feels he is created, if it flows in a natural vein, what could be wrong about it? And are there not thousands all over the world who feel attracted similarly?

Why then should paedophilia draw flack from the law and psychoanalysts, while homosexuality and other such obsessions or bondages not? The principles involved, the dynamics of how these 'natural urges' work, are the same.

Obviously, since the recipients of such pedophiliac abuse are children; children who are innocent, who are preyed upon, who can be mortally wounded physically, emotionally, mentally and even spiritually; the law goes all out to protect them.

The sad truth is that as a result of the violence inflicted upon them, these same children could become gay homosexuals or lesbians, which will receive acceptability as being "The Way I Am". Or they might crave for pre-marital sex, abort many babies, revolve around a number of relationships; and it will all be legally acceptable.

But if they turn out to be paedophiles again (which is most likely the case), then they will be considered criminals, mentally deranged and law-breakers.

This is the lie they begin to believe. This is the deception they begin to live in.

Or is it to be treated purely as a human weakness, a human failing, a frailty of stupendous proportions. Is it only a matter of breaking the law?

Yet, what happened in France, did it not leave a bitterness, a taste of disgust and horror. Did it not bring into question the level of depravity and debauchery that man could fall into? Did the ones found guilty, feel in any way a sense of sin, a sense of offence towards God and those little children?

Did anyone try to discover why? How was it at all possible for this group of people to commit such dastardly acts? What led them to it? What was at the root? What need in their inner spirits could be so great, so controlling, so compelling?

There is something much more than human frailty at stake here. There is something deeper, something vicious. An evil in the whole episode, an evil of corrupted minds and hearts, a wickedness, an abominable SIN. *No law can master such a situation*. No law is powerful enough to permeate the spirit and spiritual forces. Unfortunately, the world has yet to learn this and realize that **the law of a land, can in no way replace the law of God.** The law of the land has to be submissive to and the executive of, the law of God.

And this truth would apply to the following: the practice of homosexuality, paedophilia, masturbation, illegitimate sex, addictions to pornography, alcohol, tobacco, drugs, gambling; all of which would fall under the definition of obsessions and bondages. The root of these obsessions, the abnormalities and horrors in personages such as Hitler, Saddam, Fritzl, Marc Dutroux of Belgium and a host of others, however strange it might seem, can be located in the formative years of the persons life i.e., nine months in mother's womb and the next seven or eight years of life. However, *choosing to practice them as a way of life*, regular abuse of self and others over a period of time, would then lead to an obsession or bondage.

Those who realize that this is not the way they want to be, nor is it the way they were meant to be, with comparative ease can take recourse to counsel and or prayer and expect change and healing to take place. Because they need it and they want it.

For others, realization of the truth has to set in, before any kind of healing programme can be attempted. Progress will take place only to the extent the person is convinced it is wrong, and therefore convinced that he wants and needs the change and healing.

Chapter Eleven

TAKING CHARGE

At this stage let us recap the main principles we have established thus far:

1. Like Zacchaeus who has been used as a symbol of the hurting world, you are a hurting person. You are hurt psychologically and emotionally, bearing the scars of life upon your soul, your spirit, your body.

2. Your hurts have been imparted to you at different stages and moments of growth in life – as early as before you were born and possibly even from the moment of conception within your mother's womb.

3. With time, these hurts have lodged deep within; taken hold and claimed a major influencing role in your physical, emotional and spiritual growth. They have shaped your character, moulded your personality, controlled your behaviour, ruled your relationships and cut to size your self-worth.

4. The effect and influence that these hurts display in your life can be seen today – in abnormal behaviour patterns, in broken personality traits, in depression and suicidal tendencies, in ill health, broken children and families; in rejection of God and His laws and in an endless searching to fill in all the gaps.

5. While one may consciously be able to remember and relive many hurtful situations, what has the greater impact and power to influence our lives, are those hurts lying within the confines of the subconscious and more

so, the unconscious. It is important therefore to identify, understand and deal with these situations.

Moving Ahead

1. *Realization.* Hopefully by now you have grown into an awareness of your hurting self. You can identify areas in your personality and behaviour, your marriage, your extended friendships and relationships. You can recall with greater perceptivity not only those who have hurt you but also those whom you have hurt.

2. *Taking Responsibility.* You are willing to admit:

   - I am hurting. I am hurting others. I do not wish to leave a legacy of brokenness to my children and family. I certainly would wish the best for them.

   - No more games. No more blaming others. No more blaming parents and foster parents. No more blaming God.

   - I and I alone am responsible for my life and what is left of it. And only I can do anything about it. No one else can do it for me.

   - There must be a higher plan and purpose, a more noble calling to my life. Let me help make, if not the world, at least my own life and home, a better place.

   - I have it in me and I can do it.

3. *Forgiving the wrong done to you.* To be open and willing to forgive all who have wounded you is the beginning to all healing and peace. No matter what they may have done to you, no matter what damage they have inflicted upon you. Being so important in itself, three whole chapters are devoted to it. To forgive those who have hurt you is the key to this entire book. Equally important is to forgive yourself.

4. *Repairing the wrong you have done to others* (which often is a result of hurt). You acknowledge in humility that you may have robbed, cheated or used others; whether for personal

gain, business or sexual gratification. You have wounded others through words and actions and attitudes. You have offended them through judgements and criticisms, through gossip and slander. You have rejected others, dominated and controlled them, abused and manipulated them for your own ends; they being spouse, children, colleagues at work, friends.

Extract of Testimony:

...While doing the Forgiveness Therapy, aware of how much others had hurt me, it slowly dawned on me how much I had hurt many others as well.

... I come from a very simple rural home. At present, whatever I do is not accepted by my parents and what they do is not accepted by me. Communication with my mum has always been a problem but especially because she speaks the vernacular and I only speak English to my students (past 17 years). I don't get the words at times which irritates her tremendously. Often she shuts me up in front of my wife and daughter.

Having attended the programme I realized who and why I had to forgive.

1) *My mum was terribly worried "what would people say?" if I turned out to be another girl.*

2) *I was a late speaker. Age two and I could not say a word as yet. Being from a village and rural area they did not know any better. So my dad took a live sparrow, holding me tight forced it into my mouth for about 5 seconds. Finally I spoke as fast as I could and till today no body understands what I am saying!*

3) *My sister stiched me a trouser for a cousin's wedding and stitched on fancy buttons. Everyone laughed at me saying I was a girl.*

4) *We had a very small rural home. Around the age of 8 when my parents would have their intimacy with one another, I felt/heard mummy's voice of pain and*

sensed dad's powerful force. I would think being a man
and a wife was very cruel and I would never want to
sleep with a woman. The next day of course all was
well with them and it left me confused.

This would necessitate therefore, actually making contact where practically possible, with those whom you have hurt, asking their pardon and taking steps to correct the wrong you have done to them.

If for example you have abused your neighbour with words and accusations, it would be incumbent for you to apologize and beg his forgiveness. If you have cheated your business partner, you would be expected to make it up to him. If you have been unfaithful to your wife, you would have to climb the highest mountain to restore her faith and trust in you.

Are you willing to take this kind of action to begin the process of restoring peace within yourself, with others and with your God? Know very clearly that waiting to be judged by a court of law will not bring you freedom in your spirit, redemption from your wrong-doing, peace in your heart.

5. *Decision to love in Committed Relationships.* For those in the Eastern Hemisphere, this commitment in marriage, which for so long has been taken for granted and automatically presumed, is fast being eroded and at an alarming rate. In the Western Hemisphere it just gets worse. To remain faithful to spouse and children and aged parents, to ride all the bumps, to make time for the other, to serve and share and communicate and suffer together; calls for courage, determination and fortitude. This too has been treated separately in chapter III

Example 38: Priyanka

Piyanka first came to us a good fifteen years ago. She
was a deeply hurt person, full of fears and rejection,
believing she had a special need for attention and love. But
she readily followed our therapeutic exercises and with great
emotion and shedding of tears forgave those who had hurt
her. This went on over a period of years but strangely

enough rather than improving in physical health and over-all well-being, she seemed to deteriorate. Physical symptoms and mental depression necessitated medication, psychiatric medicine and professional counseling. Finally she had to undergo an operation for the removal of her uterus. This added to depression, as all her longings and hopes of bearing a child and becoming a mother, were dashed to the ground.

There was a long gap during which we lost contact. On resumption of Counsel and therapy, she was heard using the words "I wait to get my pound of flesh". I looked up with a start and asked for a clarification, which she confirmed. She insisted that these persons had hurt her so much that she wanted to get her revenge and placate the hurt within her. This hurt had taken place no less than twenty years earlier. "How" I asked "can bitterness and revenge go along with forgiveness therapy?"

It dawned on me that though on previous occasions she would weep bitterly and shed buckets of tears, in effect all she was doing was using these occasions as means of wallowing in self-pity. Though I would refrain from judging her true sentiments, it would seem that she had no true intentions of forgiving anyone. She had been using me and my time, to indulge herself and gain attention from me. In this case I became the scapegoat.

Wanting revenge and your pound of flesh, demanding justice by pointing fingers and condemning others; is quite the opposite of what we are aiming for through this book. Priyanka was still at the stage of blaming everyone around for her situation, her illness. She had not yet reached that stage of wanting to take responsibility, of wanting to change, of wanting to begin life anew.

Then began the direction of leading her to taking charge of her life, correcting the wrong doing, asking pardon of those she had hurt and run down, repenting before her God for offending Him, blaming Him, rebuking Him. This too did not come easy for it took long hard sessions of counsel to *convince her. She had for too long indulged herself in such attitudes and beliefs that it had taken a grip of her mind. Her thought patterns had to be reprogrammed as it were, in the right direction.*

Example 39: Yusuf

Yusuf like a million others, is another example of one who was not quite ready to take the final step that would lead to a breakthrough in his life. He was on drugs and alcohol, and often under their influence would behave boisterously, beating up his own mother, throwing her belongings out of the window and robbing whatever was left in the house, to feed his habits.

Yes, a part of him did long for freedom and healing from his bondages, thus leading him to spiritual programmes and counselling sessions. It would seem however that his taste for the old life never did leave him. A lack of perseverance and a firm decision to make a clean break, a total and complete change, regularly led him back to square one.

Taking charge of your life, by a decision to do so and setting about the right direction, is more easily said than done. Man is vain and proud. One is not going to find it easy to acknowledge one's shortcomings, one's wrongs and end up saying 'sorry'. More difficult it is for a man in charge of his office to go up to his employee and say: I am sorry I miscalculated, I should have listened to you. Or for a lady of the house (more in the eastern hemisphere) to acknowledge she was rude and disrespectful to the maid. But this is the only way to true freedom and happiness.

How easy is it for one who is wronged, beaten up, condemned unjustly and maybe even abused sexually to say to the person/s concerned "I forgive you". Can you as a strong young mind, seeking the opportunities the world has to give, prepare yourself to say to your father who has dominated/ suppressed you – I forgive you.

This is where we are at. This is what you are called to do and

196

be. Not once, but many times over. You are necessarily called to let go of your pride, your 'self-made man' attitude, your 'I don't need anybody in this world', your Macho instincts. But this is what it means to be a strong man and woman in this world. Yes, the strongest are those who can say 'sorry' and 'I forgive'. Those who are willing to eat humble pie, even though the resultant attitude from the opposite party, may be a smirk on the face.

Example 40: Bertrand

"I have been very insecure, a procrastinator and a perfectionist, judgmental, self-conscious, feeling inferior, unable to trust, unable to make decisions, having a low self-image and finally prone to self-pity."

It was pointed out that some people had made self-pity a kind of spirituality. I immediately realized that this fully applied to me. Then and there I resolved to stop wallowing in self-pity. This decision I believe:

i)   threw open the gates to look into my past objectively, not in an attitude of blaming anyone, but taking full responsibility for what I have done and what I have become (by my choices).

ii)   opened me and prepared me to accept many truths about myself, uncovered by the talks, sessions and counseling.

The last area was a difficulty to look at the past. There was a fear of reliving those painful memories. Hence the procrastination.

Most of my fears, feelings of rejections, inferiority, inability to trust, were rooted in my relationship with my father. My father had suffered from mental illness. This came to light very early in his marriage with my mother. However, circumstance saw to it that my mom and dad lived together right until his death. Thus through their marriage six children were brought into this world. I was the 4th. My dad lost his job because of his illness when I was around 5 years of age. These circumstances prevented us from experiencing parental love. Added to this, poverty and stigma due to dad's mental illness, led to great feelings of shame in the neighbourhood.

I did the forgiveness therapy with my Dad and Mom. Feelings of anger with mom surfaced as I felt her rejection. She had been unable to provide me the individual love I needed due to the number of children she had to take care of and the problems that bogged her down. The moment I did the forgiveness therapy for the childhood wounds with my mom and dad, hearing the positive things I had wanted to hear from my dad, e.g., that he loves me and was proud of me etc. I knew I had made a major breakthrough.

Finally I had to forgive my elder sister. She had been like a mother to me, yet I was hurt as my self image had been wounded gravely, by her. She had never been proud of me no matter what I did. On doing the therapy with her I knew I had crossed one more main hurdle in my path to healing.

From then on there was a new confidence in me. I began to appreciate deeply the value of the forgiveness therapy. I found myself doing the forgiveness therapy more readily for my past relationships, with a whole lot of other persons in my life.

The Parable of the Lost Son

Jesus continued: "There was a man who had two sons. The younger one said to his father, 'Father, give me my share of the estate.' So he divided his property between them.

"Not long after that, the younger son got together all he had, set off for a distant country and there squandered his wealth in wild living. After he had spent everything, there was a severe famine in that whole country, and he began to be in need. So he went and hired himself out to a citizen of that country, who sent him to his fields to feed pigs. He longed to fill his stomach with the pods that the pigs were eating, but no one gave him anything.

"When he came to his senses, he said, 'How many of my father's hired men have food to spare, and here I am starving to death! I will set out and go back to my father and say to him: Father, I have sinned against heaven and against you. I am no longer worthy to be called your son; make me like one of your hired men.' So he got up and went to his father.

"But while he was still a long way off, his father saw him and was filled with compassion for him; he ran to his son, threw his arms around him and kissed him.

"The son said to him, 'Father, I have sinned against heaven and against you. I am no longer worthy to be called your son.[a]'

"But the father said to his servants, 'Quick! Bring the best robe and put it on him. Put a ring on his finger and sandals on his feet. Bring the fattened calf and kill it. Let's have a feast and celebrate. For this son of mine was dead and is alive again; he was lost and is found.' So they began to celebrate.

In taking his share of the property and parting company with his father and family, the young man was doing no more than what many are doing today – rebelling, giving their own explanations and reasons to justify their behaviour, their relationships, their values and priorities in life; doing their own thing, making their own laws, living their own lives. Understanding it correctly, he began to live a life of debauchery.

He ended up at the bottom with nowhere to go. He was not even offered the food that the pigs were given to eat. Vs 17 says: when he came to his senses .....

The question one might ask is, how long did it take him to come to his senses. How long did it take for realization to prevail. How long before he began to take responsibility. And what were the thoughts and ideas and arguments that went through his mind before?

Is it first possible that he began grumbling at God like many probably do, in times of distress? "God what have I done so wrong that you should punish me. I harmed no one. I lived my own life. I stayed out of trouble." But after days, or even weeks or was it months of arguing in this way, sense dawned on him that he was not winning the argument, that God was not pandering to his hurt and disdain.

Next, as in a court of law, his argument shifted, to all those who became his so called 'friends' and joined him in his wine, women and song. He began blaming those on whom he spent his money, hoping to win their friendship and company, those who bled him white, those who robbed him and left him with the pigs when he was most in need. Because of them, he was in this god-awful mess. This time, he felt his argument was strong and convincing. But again, after another couple of weeks and months, there was no change in his status and he realized God was not listening to him.

Then his focus shifted to his own father. "The reason why I had to leave home was because Dad made me work like a slave on the farm. He was a hard task master. He barely allowed me time to breathe, meet my pals and have a couple of drinks. I had to get away from him. I felt imprisoned with a noose around my neck." But after stubbornly holding out on this argument for many more days, he realized he was still feeding the pigs.

Perhaps months and years had gone by, by then. Possibly he then held his elder brother responsible for his situation. He was a bully. He had pushed him around and made him do all the dirty work. That is why he had to leave house and home which finally led him to this situation. Again he realized perhaps days later, perhaps months later, that this argument got him nowhere. He was still feeding the pigs.

He made one last try before God, arguing that he never knew who his mother was, (as such there is no mention of his mother in the parable), he had never experienced her love, he had never seen her. That is why he was chasing after every girl in town in order to satisfy that deep inner need, to fill in the vacuum, to quench the thirst for love and acceptance. But God was still not convinced and he found himself as hungry as ever.

Finally he had to bow his head low and admit that he had made a mess of his life. He had allowed his deep inner emptiness to lead him astray and into wrong-doing and sin. He had allowed his feelings to get the better of him and lead him up the garden path. He had to come to the realization that blaming everyone else was not going to solve the problem. He had to come to the point of accepting responsibility for his life.

The strange thing is that when he did so and took steps in the right direction, he was clothed again with the best robe (love and acceptance), sandals on his feet (provision and protection), a ring on his finger (authority as a son once again) amidst great rejoicing and happiness.

Therefore taking responsibility and moving in the right direction will surely bring about peace, harmony and unity.

Extract of testimony:

...Since my childhood, my mother and I suffered much at the hands of my father. As I grew, a desire to take revenge and even kill him, grew along in me. I turned to smoking, drinking, late nights while forgetting my God. I even lost my Mother and turned against God as a result. I was mixed up. I was lost.

Finally I had the opportunity to confess my sinful lifestyle and experienced much freedom but still felt something deep down was binding me. Till I realized I had to forgive Dad for all the pain and trouble he brought upon us.

6. *Repairing the wrong done to God.* Strange but in each of the above stories, healing and wholeness came about by first correcting the wrong done to God. This becomes the key-stone on which all healing and change for the better, depends. Acknowledging your offence to God is the beginning of humility, acknowledging that He is overall in charge.

But what about all those who decide for their own reasons or experiences in life, that God does not exist. No one can bully another into believing in God. No one can force his/her own beliefs upon another. God and spirituality is necessarily someone and something, that must flow freely from the heart. For some, this belief is strong and vibrant. For others it is more ritualistic and for still others it is meaningless.

However, the effect and power of these exercises all depend upon how serious you are in attempting them; how sincere you are in looking into yourself to make this 'Examination of Conscience', how deeply you are convicted of your wrong doing. At the very least, you need to become aware of, confess and admit, the wrong done to others.

In the final analysis, you cannot fool God. Trying to fool the world, is a waste of time. You can only fool yourself. This is neatly expressed in the lyrics of a song that says: *I started a joke, and set the whole world laughing, but I didn't know that the joke was on me!!*

Hence are you willing to acknowledge that by words, your behaviour and your life styles, you have offended God and His authority in your life. You have got into a bad habit of blaming him for the world's ills, rebuking and rejecting him for his 'stringent' demands and in not so many words telling him to 'go to hell'.

Your rebellion is obvious in doing your own thing; such as illegitimate relationships, 'Intellectualized murder', freaking out on 'freedom' to say and do whatever you want and believe, rejecting him from your life and in general attempting to replace Him with yourself.

How you would go about correcting this would depend upon your concept and understanding of God, the intimacy of your relationship with Him. True and genuine peace of heart and mind can be a consequence only, of a true and genuine peace with God.

1. Some might content themselves in making amends by doing works of charity.

2. Others by reverting to prayerful meditation.

3. Islam depends upon God's mercy. For Hindus, a wash in the Holy River can bring about a cleansing of their souls.

4. Catholics for example could do so at the confessional while asking pardon for their 'sins' and believe they come out forgiven, accepted and loved.

Faith in God.

Here is where a little faith in God will help you more than you think. As much as it might go against the grain; as much as it might be contrary to the stand you have taken all your life; as much as it might give rise to a million and one objections; we are beginning to deal with the Inner man, the Inner self, the Inner spirit that makes the real you, created by this God.

Who else would understand your need better, your lonliness, your brokenness. Who else would know better how to put things right, than the designer and the artist of your life? Who else would know best how to mend the cracks? Who else would know better what has gone wrong, why and how. Who else would know best, what is the best remedy?

Finally if he has created you, He has a purpose and a reason. His reason is love. For His nature is love.

Chapter Twelve

WIPING CLEAN THE SLATE

A HURTFUL EXPERIENCE MAY HAVE TAKEN PLACE A MERE MINUTE AGO. Can one go back into time and change or undo what has been done? And how? Leave alone an emotional hurt that may have taken place while you were still within your mother's womb. Is there any way in which one can beat time? Has anyone yet been able to arrest the progress of time? Who has the power to control time? Who is able to go back into time and change the way we were and the things that have happened to us.

Except of course if you really do possess a time machine! Such as that you may find in the 'Back to the future' series of movies.

Memories will always remain. The history of our lives cannot change. Memories are lodged and recorded within our brain cells. But it is the hurt feelings attached to that memory/memories are what we can begin to deal with. The negative feelings, the feelings of rejection and loneliness, the feelings of guilt, hatred and fear; can be wiped clean from the slate of our hearts. And for this, there is only one way, through FORGIVENESS.

Every emotional hurt that takes place is as a result of a broken relationship, be it conscious or subconscious. A relationship that has become stressful, strained, cold. Hurt separates, divides, causes jealousy, suspicion, fear and rivalry. Every relationship can be equaled to a transaction; a transaction between two and more people. Something takes place to break that transaction. Invariably that something leaves a sore spot, an emotional wound; and the transaction or relationship cannot continue as before, in harmony and peace.

How then can this relationship ever be restored to its original quality of closeness and intimacy? The one way this transaction and relationship can be restored is through a process of communication, a process of listening and understanding, a process of pardoning and excusing; i.e., in other words, the process of forgiveness. Hence the ultimate goal of forgiveness is to restore peace and harmony in relationships. The relationship is far more important and takes precedence over one's pride, dignity, right or authority.

Relationships are what make up the world. Relationships are intrinsic to the existence of peoples, societies and cultures. Be it relationships of filial love, or relationships in marriage and sexual intimacy, relationships in families or extended to the neighbours and communities; there is a networking of human relationships through every level of humanity. Even diplomacy and business have their own kind of transactions and relationships.

Take away these relationships from this world we live in, and there can be no fun, no joy, no laughter, no sensitivity or caring or loving. There would be only Robots. Robots and suicide.

The human race is full of this brokenness, stress and strain, resulting in consequent sickness of body, emotions and spirit. This we have attempted presenting and explaining in the previous chapters thus far. Consequently there are many faith healers, philosophers and psychologists, god-men and gurus spanning the world, offering their brand of healing and solutions.

Some offer mantras, others offer techniques of meditation to calm the nerves, still others offer ways to control the mind and improve the memory, ways to psyche yourself to be calm and controlled in every kind of situation. When you are hurting or depressed, you are encouraged to exert your will power and be more assertive and forceful. Business Management principles offer you powerful tools for inter-personal relationships.

There is the power of positive thinking, programmes that offer peaceful surroundings and soft music; colour therapies and laughter as the best medicine. Down the road from where I live is the laughter club. You are invited to laugh your head off thereby relieving yourself of the strain that has been haunting you. Or you can try punching a pillow and thereby get rid of your pent up anger and bitterness.

I don't list the above in an attitude of contempt. Far from it. I believe the methods mentioned above and so many more not mentioned, are really and truly attempting to bring peace and harmony in a world of distrust and rancour. Each may have its own measure of success. There are some authors and books, who/which have taken the world by storm.

But I also believe that most of them if not all, begin their operations from level two, i.e., providing techniques to soothe the feelings of unrest and disquiet; teaching mental attitudes to assert self, motivate independence and self-confidence. While good in themselves and therapeutic, they may not be a complete and lasting therapy, resulting in a permanent good. Returning for follow up treatment, every once in a while, is a noted fact.

They begin from the level at which they find the patient. They do not penetrate deeper, i.e., to grass root or basic levels from which the patient operates, levels which are actually influencing/controlling them, knowingly or unknowingly. Usually no analysis is made of the given symptom. No attempt made to determine why, since when and how the patient is suffering/experiencing such illness or abnormalities.

Examples:

1. A patient suffering from migraine is brought to the doctor. Invariably the doctor will not attempt to locate the reason/cause of such migraine, whether physical, spiritual or mental. He will instead, treat it with medicine as recommended by the manuals.

2. A psychiatrist might attempt to control the symptoms of manic-depression or schizophrenia, with drugs. That is why

many patients under similar treatments feel a constant drowsiness or lethargy. But what is it that has led that person to be classified as one such? What emotional stress, strain and hurt has initiated such severe mental disorders? Treating such patients with drugs cannot be an end in itself or a lifelong prescription. The drugs may be required temporarily and until such time the patient returns to normalcy, to enable deeper counseling and permanent healing.

3. A priest in the confessional might have no other counsel to give the penitent sinner who has been unfaithful to his spouse or is a habitual liar; but to say "do not offend your God, do not sin again". Little might he realize that child hood hurts are at the root of such discrepancies in human behaviour, today.

If as we pre-suppose, a relationship is broken, we must recognize that hurt has taken place. Where hurt has taken place, healing is required so that restoration may result. If therefore A has been hurt by B, the principle that follows is that B in a moment of humility acknowledges the same and asks his pardon. A needs to respond by forgiving B. Whatever the nature of intensity or severity of the hurt and brokeness, this is the level every single person is at. Hurt and the need to forgive.

What Forgiveness is not:

For many, forgiveness is cowardly, weak, unbecoming of one's pride and status; something to be despised, an insult. Forgiveness is meant for the weird, for women and children, for guys without the guts, for those who cannot hold their own.. Forgiveness is effeminate. Without doubt there are those who consider themselves so strong, that they never get wounded. Therefore, forgiveness does not apply at all.

For others, forgiveness is clearly understood as the key to life and happiness. It is a process of eating humble pie and yet coming out stronger than before. It is a process of turning the other cheek and yet growing fuller in the face. It is a process of yielding a last bit of pride and yet being filled with a peace, confidence and security never known before.

As I write, I imagine a very common scene in a city like Mumbai (Bombay) where a taxi collides with another. The drivers will emerge at great speed, arms flaying, voices screaming, having a free-for-all in the middle of the road, oblivious to the jam-up of traffic on either side. Tempers are let loose, sleeves rolled up, threats and abuse at every second word. But why go to such a length?

Is the answer, to protect and ensure one's pride and dignity? Hence the passion displayed would merely be the sign of one's insecurity, one's fear and a cover-up for one's poor self-image. Should this happen to two executives being driven to work, hopefully they would reprimand their respective drivers, shake hands and send the bill to their respective Insurance Agencies!

What Forgiveness is:

The late Pope John Paul II visited his would-be assassin in jail, had a heart to heart chat with him and forgave him for making the attempt on his life, which left him in pain and weakness. Mrs. Gladys Staines, the Australian missionary working in India, publicly forgave those who had burnt her husband and children to death. It cost her to give up her right to anger, revenge and justice for her loved ones.

If anyone could ever imagine such an act of forgiveness was effeminate, a sign of weakness and fear, or even a compromise in a very difficult situation, they can only be pitied. Gandhi, as is shown in the movie of the same name, learned to forgive those who dominated, bullied and used strong-arm tactics. Because he was devoid of anger in his heart towards such people, he was able to use the powerful means of non-violence, which finally brought freedom to his country.

Forgiveness is that process, that act, that attitude and decision of mind and heart, to let go of one's right to anger and hatred, one's right to vengeance and vindication, one's right to hit back, one's right to justice. Forgiveness is quite the opposite of 'saving one's pride'.

To FORGIVE, by interchanging the syllables, would mean to

GIVE (be)FOR(e). To give before you can exercise your anger, your hatred or your pound of flesh. To give before the person even becomes aware of what he or she has done to you. To give before the person can even begin to ask pardon. Through forgiveness you are therefore releasing or setting free that person from your rightful rod of anger. You give even before that person can begin to change. Thus forgiveness clears the air, removes the grime and dirt from the transaction and restores peace, trust and goodness, to the relationship.

Example 41: Sharon

Sharon's relationships were twisted. They tied her up into a pretty knot. She wanted to break away and walk the right path but was frightened by the repercussions. What action would that man take if she did leave. She was afraid of him, especially since he had underworld connections and was possessive of her. On the other hand Mum had a nice young man in mind for her. But she found it difficult to say no. On all sides she was hemmed in.

Yet during our programme she learned to forgive. She truly forgave every one who had hurt her and was presently controlling her through forceful means. Before the program was even concluded, she received a message from home that every single avenue had opened up and she could return home safe with nothing to worry about.

Example 42: Sheila

Sheila had worked in a large and important Government Hospital as Warden and Supervisor of all the nurses in that hospital. She retired and awaited her retirement benefits (A regular procedure in India). She had been waiting for many years now, with no sign of the cheque. Bribes were expected but she refused to pay. Many hours were spent in travel and visiting the various offices, much money was spent in transport too, but to no avail.

Sheila learned to forgive. She forgave every officer and

clerk involved in the office that had to pay out her cheque. She forgave them for holding back her monies that were due to her. She forgave them for attempting to use their authority and power in the situation to make a quick buck for themselves. That same week she got a call from the office to come and pick up her cheque.

Forgiveness releases the power to change

The one forgiving and the one forgiven, both change in different ways. Individuals change for the better. Consequently families and neighbors can also change. Forgiveness can bring healing to body and soul and spirit. Forgiveness is perhaps the first step to growing into unity and oneness. Forgiveness is the key.

Forgiveness is required on a daily basis. Daily, there will be those standing on your corns, those saying a harsh word to you, those accusing you unjustly, those robbing you of your dignity, good name and integrity. Daily, we retire to bed grumpy, uneasy, exhausted. You begin the next day, deceiving yourself that all is fresh and anew, not realizing or accepting that the transactions of yesterday and the day before, continue to prod, poke and irritate.

Little does one realize the benefit of consciously bringing the persons responsible for your grumpiness, before you, to impart forgiveness to them. This results in a peace beyond description. Each day truly begins as a new day. At work, you will find your relationships healthy and positive, your efficiency, improving.

Some common obstacles to Forgiveness

1. *I never keep hurt inside me.* Some are under the mistaken illusion that while they might have a quick temper, they never keep hurt/animosity/for long. Or perhaps for just those few moments they might lose their shirts and after, they are perfectly at peace. If this is true, all credit to you. But the human race is more sensitive and susceptible than imagined. Hence such an attitude would more likely deceive than be realistic. An actual process of forgiveness, assisting one to recall and relive hurtful memories will be the true test.

2. *Denial.* Denial that you are even hurt; denying that the harsh and cruel treatment metered out to you by your tyrannical father has left no scars or wounds upon you; becomes an escapism. Fear prevents you from looking at the truth, because the truth is too painful to handle. Pride would also dictate that 'no matter how bad my father was, it has not affected me in the least.' One needs to let go of this in all humility and learn to accept...

3. *I won't forgive until ...* Putting conditions to your forgiveness will not bring peace, for that will not be true forgiveness. Forgiveness necessarily demands no conditions or limits. The very meaning and nature of forgiveness is such, that it does not depend upon what the other person is thinking, feeling or planning to do. Forgiveness must flow freely and without limit.

4. *Must I forgive every single time?* Each relationship is like a link in a chain. For that chain to remain strong and useful, each link needs to be strong. The weak link in the chain can jeopardize the whole chain. As the saying goes: A chain is as strong as its weakest link. This is what might happen when even one relationship may remain weak because you are not prepared to forgive.

5. *What if I am willing to forgive but not so the other?* More often than not, the other party may not be in a forgiving or receiving mood. Your attempts to forgive might be met with a slammed door. The other may despise you even more, turning on you with wrath and anger. Well, you should be satisfied that you have made the effort, you have done your bit. Irrespective of how the other might act, your forgiveness counts.

6. *I have forgiven but I cannot forget.* We have already clarified that memories will never be wiped away. It is the hurt attached to those memories that we are dealing with. Hence while you have forgiven sincerely and truly, the memory will always remain. But if even after forgiving, the memory still troubles you, irks you, remains a raw spot; then

that might be a sign that forgiveness is not complete and you need to repeat the process.

When true forgiveness sets in, the memory will no longer trouble you. In fact, you will see it as a means of refinement into maturity. Gradually but surely it will be pushed into the confines of the subconscious.

7. *I want to forgive but I cannot.* Sometimes a person is bound. No matter how much he/she may desire to forgive, something seems to hold him back. Often this is due to past and unresolved issues. If for example, you have not yet forgiven a very deep and sensitive issue when you were a child; or you have withheld forgiveness to another; or in analyzing a particularly painful incident of the past you have now come to realize that you have all these years held the wrong person accountable for your situation. This lack of forgiveness remains as a bondage, binds you and acts as a block to all further attempts to forgive. Dealing with these situations through forgiveness will release you to forgive today.

A thought to chew on

Today it is not uncommon to speak of and encourage the phenomenon of forgiveness. Every now and then articles appear in the newspapers upholding its advantages. Counsellors encourage their patients to do so. Health and Stress experts advise the benefits of forgiveness in attaining a "happy state of affairs", the idea being to rid one of any unwanted baggage.

However the big question is – Do they all have the same understanding of the term Forgiveness. Are they aware of its true context and origins. Do they realize it's wider purpose, it's scope, it's meaning. Is their understanding of the term subjective, or have they acquired their understanding from the originator?

Where then did this concept of forgiveness first begin. When did it first originate. What was the context directly relating to its development. Who is responsible for such an idea?

A phrase in the English language and coined by Alexander Pope reads like this: *"To err is human, to forgive is Divine"*. Pope, in all probability, received his inspiration from the following incident.

There is the story of the paralytic who is lowered down through the roof to be healed by Jesus. Jesus says to him "My child, your sins are forgiven". This caused an uproar among the scribes and the Pharisees present, who retorted, "Who does this man think he is? *"Only God can forgive sins"*.

Forgiveness does not come normal to man. Man is not blessed with a natural inclination or desire to forgive. It is not inbuilt or automatic for man to be led to forgive, in any given situation. On the contrary, he is automatically led to defend, blame, fight and destroy. And this has been the history of the development and destruction of the world. As the commentary on this phrase says *"To forgive is Divine, but to get even is human"*.

Forgiveness is beyond normal thinking man and his behaviour. Forgiveness is not a human trait. Forgiveness is beyond the scope of human man. Forgiveness is not a man-idea. Forgiveness needs to be learned.

No man, no god-man, no person of holiness, no guru of enlightenment has ever spoken of or taught the idea of forgiveness. No religion or philosophy has ever conceived such a phenomenon or thought-pattern in its originality.

The originator of this thought is in the Bible. Jesus is the one person, man or God as you may wish to believe, who lived it, taught it and died with it upon his lips and heart. Forgiveness is supernatural. Forgiveness is a God –thought. Forgiveness is a God idea. Only a loving God could conceive such a thing.

If you desire therefore to live this line of forgiveness, to receive healing and peace of mind, it *may* make sense to learn more about this phenomenon, from the *Man* himself.

But this does not mean that you have to embrace Christianity in order to begin to forgive. You can begin your forgiveness process right here and now, as long as you accept the concept, the meaning and its purpose. As long as you realize you need God's help, as you cannot forgive by your own power. As long as your desires, motives and objectives are clean and pure.

And this would also apply to those who do not believe in God. The nature of forgiveness is such that in some mysterious way its power to heal and unite is released. This happens when you desire to heal the relationship, when you have a keenness to build a community of love and wholeness, when you sincerely search to live the truth, when you realize and are aware that, man has a higher calling than to live in brokenness and depravity.

✳ ✳ ✳

Prelude to Chapter Thirteen

Hence, if you sincerely desire to understand the true significance and power of forgiveness, if you wish to walk down that road to a deeper experience of healing and wholeness, if you desire to embrace that higher calling, plan and purpose for mankind, you must understand it from a Christian perspective, in the following chapter.

The idea of this chapter is not to be religious, spiritual or evangelical. The idea is to make available the benefits of true forgiveness, to the reader and in fact to the whole world. In many ways, the world is in shambles. The world can do with all the possible help it can get, to be more wholesome and a better place to live in.

Chapter Thirteen

FORGIVENESS, A CHRISTIAN PERSPECTIVE

You may have heard the expression "An eye for an eye and a tooth for a tooth" and you may have simply understood it as "Tit for Tat". But this phrase of English literature actually had its origins in the ancient law of Babylonia commonly known as Hammurabi's law. The Jewish people lived by the law that God had given to them. The law provided guidelines in order to live lives of order, unity and justice.

Apart from guidelines for the conduct of their personal lives, the law even told them how to conduct themselves with others, with friends, with their enemies. If for example one was robbed of one hundred units by a neighbour, partner in business or the grocer; the law would permit you to take back from that person, with force if need be, only one hundred units, not a penny more nor a penny less. That would be accounted for as justice. To the extent that you were hurt, wounded, robbed; to that extent and not more could you return the same.

If the neighbour's sheep dog killed and destroyed three of your livestock, you were permitted to do the same to three of his. Not a sheep more. For that would be unjust. The punishment had to fit the crime!

But what would happen in a case where two men were involved in a brawl and one beat up the other, knocking out one tooth of his. Invariably as is common with human nature, the other would wait for the opportune moment, hit back with force and vengeance, thereby knocking out two or more of his opponent's teeth.

This in the eye of the law was unjust as one ended up more severely hurt than the other. Especially if one was more powerfully built, the other was sure to get the worst of it. Hence the law provided a safety clause. If you knocked out one tooth from your neighbour, only one of yours could be knocked out.

Laughable in today's world perhaps, but nevertheless an attempt to maintain order and justice, some four thousand years ago, in man's simple, nomadic and limited lifestyle.

Today, the Christian understanding of Forgiveness goes much beyond this almost feudal concept of Mercy and Justice. Let us take the parable of the unforgiving debtor from the Gospel of Matthew Chapter 18 vs. 23 to 35.

The Unforgiving Debtor

"Therefore, the kingdom of heaven is like a king who wanted to settle accounts with his servants. As he began the settlement, a man who owed him ten thousand talents was brought to him. Since he was not able to pay, the master ordered that he and his wife and his children and all that he had be sold to repay the debt.

"The servant fell on his knees before him. 'Be patient with me,' he begged, 'and I will pay back everything.' The servant's master took pity on him, cancelled the debt and let him go.

"But when that servant went out, he found one of his fellow servants who owed him a hundred denarii. He grabbed him and began to choke him. 'Pay back what you owe me!' he demanded.

"His fellow servant fell to his knees and begged him, 'Be patient with me, and I will pay you back.'

"But he refused. Instead, he went off and had the man thrown into prison until he could pay the debt. When the other servants saw what had happened, they were greatly distressed and went and told their master everything that had happened.

"Then the master called the servant in. 'You wicked servant,' he said, 'I cancelled all that debt of yours because you begged me to. Shouldn't you have had mercy on your fellow servant just as I had on you?' In anger his master turned him over to the jailers to be tortured, until he should pay back all he owed.

"This is how my heavenly Father will treat each of you unless you forgive your brother from your heart."

The King settling his accounts with his servants, firstly is a symbol of God settling accounts in heaven. A man is brought to the King. This man owes the King the equivalent of 3,000,000 pound sterling, which today in itself is a mighty fortune. Two thousand years ago this amount might be the equivalent of some 6,00,000,000 pounds, calculating inflation at approximately 10 per cent annually.

At its deeper meaning, the story uses the example of material money and property to bring out the much more serious message of salvation. Man is in a Spiritual Debt to God to such an astronomical extent that there is absolutely no way he could ever pay back. There is absolutely no way he could extricate himself out of this mess. There is no way he could save himself.

What Is This Spiritual Debt?

Essentially man has been hurt by other men, as we have already studied in quite a bit of detail. This hurt has left a deep void. Now begins a process of filling up this void. Man is left with a choice. Either he can fill up this void by:

1. Forgiving those who have hurt him and allow God's love to penetrate the void of his heart to substitute for all that is missing, by way of love, acceptance and self worth.

   OR

2. By accepting the lure and enticements of the world; by satiating his selfish desires and appetites; by inviting the devil to fill in that void. Satanic worship is more prevalent than one might be willing to acknowledge. The last

217

paragraph, Dynamics of Hurt, in Chapter Eight, will help bring home this truth.

Man has made a decision and chosen to be led by his feelings, his emotions, his ego. He has chosen the second alternative. He has chosen to do things the way he sees them. He has made the choice to be his own boss, the choice not to let anyone tell him what he should do, the choice to be in control of his own life.

This, is the essence of Sin. Man in his pride and disobedience, has turned away from his God and Creator. Man has rebuffed God; His relationship with Him, His daily presence and love, His authority in his life. Man has slapped God in the face and said:

"I no longer need you, I can manage on my own. Your demands and rules for living are obsolete, a hindrance to growth and freedom, regressive. Therefore I shall inspire and install my own philosophy, rules and directives".

Not realizing perhaps, the full implications of what he was doing, Man became 'god'. By choosing to reject God, man chooses eternal death and everlasting punishment. The effect or fruit of his choice on this earth, is Hatred, Envy, Lust, Perversity, Selfishness, Greed, Fear, Loneliness, Brokenness, Sickness and the like.

This choice, this sin and its effect, has penetrated the whole human race. *Man has chosen by his own Free Will, eternal damnation and separation from God.* There was therefore no hope for Man. And nothing man can try of his own; no amount of social work or uplift, no new philosophy, no meditations, no mantras, nothing can save him. Man has condemned himself to eternal death. This is the spiritual debt, he has landed himself in.

The first great truth

But God's love is infinite and He cannot let go of His prized creation, Man, whom He has created in His own Image and Likeness. He will not let his plan be thwarted by Man's foolishness and deception or any interference by satanic powers. He goes still a step further, sends His son Jesus to save mankind and the world, by his death.

Jesus, by his life and example; through his ministry of teaching, healing and miracles; by his suffering, passion and crucifixion; showed complete obedience to God's Will, doing exactly as God would have him do. Often Jesus would tell his disciples "I come, not to do my own Will, but my Father's Will". At Gethsemane in prayer he would say "Father, if it is possible, let this Chalice pass by me, nevertheless, not my Will, but thy Will be done". Indicating, his total surrender to and acceptance of the Will of God his Father.

By so doing, Jesus has done the exact opposite of what man had done in using his free will in the wrong way. He has countered perfectly the effect of that choice that man has made against God and his plan. He has turned 180 degrees, turning back towards God.

That is why on his cross he could now say, "Father, forgive them, for they know not what they do". By his total obedience, he had won forgiveness for the world's sin. As his reward for being totally obedient to His Heavenly Father, he could now claim forgiveness for man's foolishness, in rejecting and offending God. He was now in a position to restore all that man had lost through selfishness, greed and pride.

You can imagine the following conversation with His Father:

"I have done it all, as you wanted me to do. Dotted every "i" and crossed every "t", having left nothing undone. In so doing I have won for them your forgiveness. I have earned it on their behalf. Without me they wouldn't have had a chance. After all, they were so caught up in their selfishness, that they were blinded to the consequences and ramifications of their actions, decisions and beliefs.

Now, what is remaining to finish the job, is your forgiveness of them. Now it is time for your response, your action. Your mercy. Let it be my reward for being totally obedient to your Will. So that I can finally say "It is accomplished".

This is how he won salvation for the world. He did it through forgiveness. In other words:

1. Forgiveness = Salvation

By forgiving us our sin, he is saving us from the effect of our sin. He saves us from the effect of our choices. He saves us from eternal death and punishment. He releases us from the bondage of sin and evil so that we may live the abundant life. Like the Prodigal Son who had renounced his sonship and all that went with it, i.e., life, happiness, wealth, authority; but who returned in repentance; God restores to man all that he had lost.

The purpose of the parable is for the believer to realize how great a debt he has been forgiven. And funnily, due to no credit of his own. He did nothing to earn this forgiveness. He could do nothing to earn this salvation. He deserved nothing. It was purely the magnanimous gesture of the great King. A free gesture of the King, in just brushing aside this great debt.

In chapter 12 we have an explanation for "To err is human, to forgive is divine." This is what Christianity believes. Only God can forgive sins. For only God can be God to do such wondrous things. Since Sin is an affront to God, since Sin is a rejection of God, since Sin is something committed against God; only God can respond to it and do something about it. He chooses to Forgive. And in so doing, he chooses to Save.

No other god-man or guru or religious belief has spoken of the concept of forgiveness. Forgiveness seems to be the monopoly of Christianity. Forgiveness is at the heart and soul of Christianity. Forgiveness is the very core of the Christian Faith. Forgiveness is Salvation.

Jesus demands the same from each one. And therefore to be able to forgive in the truest sense of the term means to forgive only in and through God, in and through Jesus.

Wouldn't one therefore and normally expect this man to forgive his fellow servant the small loan of 100 denarii, the equivalent of 5 pound sterling. In today's value that might be the equivalent to 1000 pound sterling, only. Again the point in question is not the amount itself, but the difference between the two figures.

Whatever others may have robbed us of, the debt that others owe us, the hurt others have given us, the emotional wounds of rejection and pain that has dominated the pages of this book; is a drop in the ocean compared to the resulting offence that we have given God. What is our response going to be towards them? Are we going to condemn and bind them by not forgiving them, by not releasing them, by holding back our pardon and waiting to get our pound of flesh?

That is what the parable speaks of. It is not worth it, to take the second alternative mentioned above. The second one speaks of certain Death to the inner life, the inner spirit that God has breathed into us. The first alternative speaks of salvation and life. A life and peace that only God can provide.

Hence what the Bible teaches is that, if any believer of Christ wants salvation and forgiveness for his sin, he must necessarily search his heart to consciously and willingly forgive those who have hurt him, no matter how deep, how painful, how humiliating. Otherwise he needn't waste his time and expect God to do something for him, when he cannot follow the basic spiritual law. This idea is emphasized by Jesus himself, in the prayer that he taught his followers.

The Our Father. The line that we focus upon says – "forgive us our sin as we forgive those who sin against us" – The implications of this prayer are clear. If we are not prepared to forgive, if we are not prepared to try, if we are not prepared to even take a first step in forgiving those who have hurt us, we are telling God in fact not to forgive us our sin and wrong doing. We in fact close our hearts to His forgiveness and salvation.

The Bible, through many other passages strengthens this idea to such an extent, making forgiveness the greatest demand of the Christian Faith. For example Jesus says in the Gospel of Matthew Chapter Five vs. 23 *"So then, if you are bringing your offering to the altar and there remember that your brother has something against you, leave your offering ....go be reconciled to him ... then come back and make your offering"*.

One can understand the demand if you yourself had some ill feeling against your brother. It makes sense therefore, to clear your heart of animosity and ill-will before offering your gift at the Altar. But if your conscience is clear, you have nothing against anyone, your heart is clean; how can it become your responsibility to reconcile/restore the relationship, if your brother/someone else is upset with you for some unknown reason?

This is how strongly the Bible looks at broken relationships. Christianity does not spare her followers in any way. No one is excused or exempted from this demand. The responsibility is always yours. There is no room for pointing fingers. There is no room for blaming anymore. For the simple reason that, you are a special creation of God and he has a special plan for you.

A plan in every way much more superior than the life he has given to other living creatures. A plan of harmony, peace and oneness in unity, just as God himself is harmoniously one, Father, Son and Holy Spirit. This is His ultimate plan for Man, his very special creation. To be one in mind and heart and spirit in marriage first, then with all peoples; just as God Himself is One.

The second great truth

And now we come to an even more interesting truth. The realization that, when we forgive others the hurt they have caused us, are we merely conveying a human forgiveness? Are we merely restoring a human relationship? Are we doing it only because He demands it? Or do we realize that:

2. When we forgive others, we are passing on salvation as well, to them.

We are not passing on human forgiveness, for there is no such thing. Forgiveness is divine. Forgiveness is Godly in nature. Forgiveness is salvation and therefore we become partners with Christ in saving the world. We become his instruments in passing salvation from one to another. We can begin a process of 'forgiving and saving' those who desperately need it, those who might not realize they need it or want it, those who may not know where to look for it, even those who might not want to believe in Jesus.

THE DIAMOND OF CHRISTIAN FORGIVENESS

Forgiveness can be compared to a diamond in many ways.

1. A Diamond is formed in the bowels of the earth, under tons of pressure, over the years. Forgiveness arises from the inner heart of man, from the filth and muck of hurt and its consequences.

2. A Diamond when cut and polished, brings sparkle and beauty. Forgiveness, given and received, brings life and peace.

3. A Diamond is hard enough to cut through and polish. Forgiveness is the only virtue that is tough enough to cut through hurt, insensitivity, obsessions and compulsive habits, evil, wickedness and sin.

4. A Diamond may be a rich woman's best friend. Forgiveness is for the world.

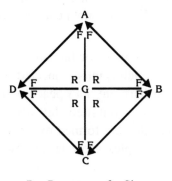

R = Repentance for Sin
F = Forgiveness for Sin

Forgiveness cannot be acquired by proxy, through a power of attorney, an sms, by popular vote, in a group or on the Internet.

Each person seeking God's forgiveness, approaches individually in a spirit of repentance for all sin and wrong-doing. God saves, redeems each one individually again, by granting forgiveness. Thus each receives personal salvation and grace.

In turn each believer is called to forgive his neighbour, thereby passing on to that neighbour the same forgiveness received from God. In other words we pass on to another the salvation and power of God's forgiveness. This is the plan of God, that each one becomes a partner with Him in forgiving and thereby saving the other. This is the very life of God available at our fingertips.

When a person decides not to be open to giving or receiving forgiveness, when a person refutes another's offer of reconciliation, he is in fact building a wall around himself, a wall of Jericho. He is cutting himself off from others and therefore from God too. He is closing his fist, his heart, to God as well.

For, if in this stage he seeks forgiveness from God for his sin, his failings, his wrong-doing, God will not forgive him, as stated by Jesus himself, in the verse immediately following the Our Father. Which in a practical way means – he is unable to receive of God's forgiveness because of a closed heart, a clenched fist. God's forgiveness and love cannot penetrate through that wall of Jericho.

Thus we see the network of human relationships we were talking about earlier. Each is interconnected, each is forgiven by the other, each is in harmony and peace with the other as the cycle of forgiveness is pursued day after day. This cycle becomes like ripples that are formed by throwing a stone into a pond of water. The ripples grow larger and larger spreading outwards.

This is what it could be like when each one forgives another and he in turn forgives still another and another and another. A wave of God's power begins to flow. A revolution of forgiveness and love rises up. A revolution, that can and will change the world and make it a haven of peace.

But to reach that goal is going to take a whole lot of forgiving back and forth, seventy times seven. If man is able to reach the moon and outer space, if man is able to make a clone, if man is able to communicate through space age technology, surely it is not beyond the scope of man's ability to create a world of forgiveness and loving people - with God's help.

FORGIVENESS FOR THE NATIONS

Forgiveness begins on a one-to-one level. But it is also necessary on a communitarian level where families have to forgive each other for years of feuds, hatred, prejudice and bigotry.

Managing Committees in business, society and even local Church set-ups, require accountability and forgiveness for showing partiality, unfairness, injustice and racism.

Communities forgive communities for black-white prejudice, which may still continue till date. Races, creeds and religions forgive those who have attacked, enslaved and persecuted them.

Nations and governments need to open their eyes to their folly, bullying tactics and selfish ambitions. The United Nations brings a semblance of order and justice among them, but cannot heal the wounds permanently to establish genuine unity and peace.

Terrorists may always exist and be hunted down for fighting their causes with a 'just war'. If hunter and hunted could seek deeper understanding and forgiveness of each other, forgiveness of a Herculean nature; for wounds, violent death and injustices meted out; who would have need to fear walking down their streets? Who would have need of territorial borders?

Regrettably-there may always remain hard-nosed, stiff-necked people who are afraid and threatened by the negotiation table.

What then is there to stop Hindus, Muslims and Christians from working hand in hand? Who is going to differentiate between black and white, rich or poor, developed and underdeveloped?

What about past conflicts between communities and countries that have inflicted mental, spiritual and emotional wounds and infestations upon future generations? Such as the Holocaust, the Black-White discrimination in America, the IRA-led violence in the UK, the Hindu-Muslim riots of India, the blood-spilling between tribes of Africa, the hatred between Croats and Serbs.

The horrors of these events have only partly been depicted through Hollywood and hang like dark clouds over those nations. Which country, which continent, does not need healing of some kind or the other?

Is the Healing of Nations a possibility or is it a far-fetched dream.

CAN OUR DREAM OF ONE UNITED NATION BECOME A REALITY?

Chapter Fourteen

FORGIVENESS THERAPY

The main goal of the Forgiveness Therapy is to evacuate the hurt feelings lying within yourself, followed by forgiving the person/s concerned. Other therapies encourage in different ways the releasing of steam, the expressing of anger and rage, but may not end with forgiveness. It is forgiveness that heals, that transcends this hurting transaction, making it well again. You do this by following two basic principles:

Recall

To recall simply means to remember, to remember all details possible. Where the hurt has taken place in the distant past; with the passage of time it is usually pushed under the carpet and into the realm of the subconscious. Hence recalling the memory with details brings it to life again. Remembering the look on the faces, or the colour of the shirt worn, or the furniture in the room, and such temporal details, helps the negative feelings too, to surface.

One might make the mistake of believing that it is no longer of any consequence. This might apply particularly in the case of a very gory memory, let's say for example one of sexual abuse. Today many years later, you think and feel as an adult. The memory and details of the incident are a blur. You probably feel and think that you are no longer worried by that wound and memory. After all, "Time is a Healer". You need to put yourself in the shoes of that little boy or girl you once were.

The subconscious mind tries its best to forget those experiences which are not acceptable, not pleasant, not happy. It is only natural that the mind tries to shut out, water down, and cause such memories to fade away. As the memories fade away, so also the awareness of the feelings attached to those memories. Remembering, therefore, in this case, the sexual hurt: remember your age, what you looked like, what you might have been wearing, who came along, how he or she enticed you. Face what the person actually did to you. And you will be surprised what comes up from the emotional level.

There are also those experiences which might lie deep in the unconscious. Consciously you might not feel anything, you might not be aware of the implications. But you remember what parents and others told you, about what happened when you were one year old, or just born, or even while in your mother's womb. This is where you have to take the cue from what you were told, or what you have come to understand from Chapter VI 'Getting to the Heart of Things' and let your imagination run loose.

Imagine what Mum did go through and how it might have affected you. Imagine, if be, what you went through in mother's womb during those days and times. Imagine yourself as a little curled up fetus subject to the whims and fancies of mum, dad and surroundings. The subconscious somehow directs the imagination and the fuller picture unfurls.

Relive

Allow the hurt feelings to surface. Get in touch with them. These are the trouble spots. Here lies the poison that is eating into you and destroying you. It is the negative feelings and not merely the memory, that, lying hidden and suppressed, cause us the many troubles and difficulties we have been talking about. Do not let these negative feelings overpower you by causing you to run away and shut the memory out. Face these feelings. Be aware that this is you.

I refer to my own example and testimony in Chapter XV. I myself used this method from the moment I got stuck i.e. after I fell asleep with the anesthesia. How could I ever remember what happened next. How could I ever know what happened, while I was in an unconscious state. I began to imagine, based on what my parents and others had told me. My subconscious took over.

Example 43: Jennifer

Jennifer was suffering from guilt because she had aborted a child. As she was led into this imagination exercise, she expressed her guilt to her little baby, asked her baby's forgiveness, told her how much she missed her and loved her, how she was very much part of the family. After completing the exercise and accepting baby's forgiveness, she seemed to visualize herself walking along with her baby to a high wall. The baby entered this enclosure saying good-bye. Jennifer could hear the happy sounds of children at play.

Finally there are those who have cut themselves off from their feelings such that, though they follow the Forgiveness Therapy, sincerely from their heart and mind, they will not feel a thing. There will be no expression of emotions. There will be no sign of tears, no sign of hurts being expelled, but just an empty recalling of memories. This usually is because of a situation/s so deep and painful that your heart gets used to the idea of hurt, there being nothing you can do about it.

Example 44: Amina

Amina recounts some very deep and painful memories but in a mechanical and matter-of-fact sort of way. The things she has gone through amazes me and makes me wonder how people (how parents, educated by worldly standards) can be so stupid and foolish. Normally one might expect buckets of tears to accompany such a tale. But with Amina there was a dryness beyond belief.

It turned out that when she was a young girl of five and six, the maid employed to look after her and the home, would regularly lock her up in the toilet to avoid being troubled. The maid would not feed her or look after her, the

*maid would entertain herself with the T.V. and with
her men friends.*

*When Mum and Dad returned home from work,
Amina would recount to them what the maid had done.
As young as she was, she knew something was amiss
when she heard the voices of other strange men in the
house. Amina without doubt would express her feelings,
tears, fears and upset with the maid. But the moment
her mother took it up with the maid, the maid would
silently climb upon a stool, take her suitcase down from
the loft and prepare to pack and leave. Soon Amina
would see her mum begging and pleading with the maid
not to leave. In fact she even recalled her mother on
bended knee 'crying out for mercy' as it were.*

'Why such obtuse behaviour? It turned out that the mother's
job meant everything to Amina's mother. Whether it was her
career, her social standing with others in the neighbourhood, the
financial situation at home; her job was the most important to her.
Her job ultimately was more important than Amina herself. She
could not let anything jeopardize her job. But if it meant some
inconvenience to her daughter, that was acceptable.

And this is the message Amina got the first time she
complained. This is the message that was pushed home and
ingrained into her day after day. Gradually the tears dried up. The
situation at home became a daily normal routine, about which
Amina could do nothing. There was no point in complaining.
There was nothing she could do about the situation. She just had
to grin and bear it.

The tears, the distrust of her mother and emotional blackmail
was buried deep inside. This kind of situation takes a lot of talking
out, trying to express the feelings. The tears have to be poked at.
Sometimes the only way for the dam to break, is to be rough and
harsh with the person.

This process of Recalling and Reliving is activated when you
go through the following steps of what we call the Forgiveness
Therapy.

STEP 1: To Accuse the person in love

1. *Be Alone.* Retire to your room, your hiding place, a quiet corner under a tree or wherever you can be alone, secluded from everybody else. No one else especially the persons you are dealing with, must be anywhere near. The only exception can be that person who knows your background, who is in some capacity your counsellor, who is supporting you in this effort.

2. *Be Detailed.* Sit in a chair and place another empty chair opposite and facing you. Imagine the person who has hurt you and whom you plan doing the therapy with, is sitting in the chair opposite. Begin to tell that person how he or she has hurt you, by recalling the memories. Recount the details. Memories surface because no matter how tiny and unimportant they might seem, they have had an effect upon you, they are ready at this moment for healing.

3. *Evacuate.* As you recall the memories, recall the hurt feelings and negative experiences attached. Describe what you went through. How you felt, how you squirmed, how it disgusted you, the anger and hate that arose, the fear. Tell that person how that action of his or hers is affecting you even today. If anger wells up, express it. If questions arise, ask them. At times I even permit a person to use abusive, if this helps to describe more fully and completely the feelings. This is the step of emptying out, of spilling out the beans, of vomiting out the feelings, the memories, the suppressed tears, fears, words, etc. Leave no stone unturned, however small and trifling it may seem.

4. *Do it audibly.* Some, for whatever reason, believe doing it audibly is unnecessary especially when they find it difficult to find a place where they can be all by themselves. Do it in your mind and it will not have any effect. When you do it audibly, you are best able to describe what is in you, even better than putting it on paper. At a minimum, do it softly, under your breathe but mouth the words.

STEP 2: The Accused asks for forgiveness

When the first step is over and you feel you have nothing more to say, you have evacuated all the poison from within, change chairs and sit in the opposite chair. You now take the place of the accused, imagining you yourself are seated across, i.e., in the first chair. Now you speak, again and always audibly, as the accused, to yourself seated opposite. What would you want the accused to say? How would you want the accused to respond. Do not speak what you expect him or her to say in real life, but what you want to hear. What you need to hear.

Perhaps briefly the accused (now yourself speaking on his/her behalf) will explain from his point of view how he was ignorant of what he had done, or that was the only way he knew how to behave, or he did not mean to hurt at all, or he wanted to do his / her best and that is the only way he/she knew how to. Finally the accused asks for forgiveness.

There is no need for the accused to go into a long litany of explanations and excuses. A brief response should be enough. But you are encouraged to go ahead with details if they help you to understand the background of the accused, that is, what the circumstances of his/her childhood were. This might help you understand why the accused is the kind of person he/she is today. Understanding the hardships and sufferings a person has experienced in life, leads to compassion and makes it easier to forgive.

STEP 3: Forgive

Change chairs again and revert to your previous position. That is, you are once again the Accuser and you must imagine that the accused is in the opposite chair. Now, having emptied yourself of all hurt feelings, now understanding the accused better, forgive him/her freely and willingly. This forgiveness must not come grudgingly or with conditions. There should be no conditions of 'better not let it happen again or else ......' or ' I do not want anything to do with you anymore'. You could say something like this:

'In the name of God ... I forgive you'

'With the love of God .... I love you'

as we have come to understand that only God can forgive. Better still, if a Christian you could say:

'In the name of Jesus, I forgive.'

'With the love of Jesus, I love you'.

Make this forgiveness meaningful. Use words, use actions, use gestures to make it realistic. You could say:

'Today I realize that you did not really mean to hurt' or

'I understand what you were going through at the time' or

'I really do want to forgive you from the bottom of my heart'

Actions and gestures of walking across to the chair opposite, imagining you are lifting the accused out of the chair by the arm and hugging him/her, or shaking hands, or kissing a photograph of said person especially if a close member of your family, all helps in the process.

STEP 4: Prayer:

A prayer in faith goes a long way to make this therapy effective.

NOTE:

1. This therapy must be done audibly, i.e. loud enough to hear yourself. I repeat this because after explaining in detail the whole therapy, many continue to do it their own way, i.e., in the mind. This would be redundant and tantamount to triggering off the past hurt with no apparent healing or transformation.

2. The person you have to forgive may be dead and gone. That is immaterial, as the hurt that needs to be healed is inside you and not inside the dead person. If you were dead and gone, this therapy would not apply!

3. For most people, forgiveness still has to be given and received. But this does not necessarily mean that you yourself have not forgiven. Forgiveness is a decision of the

mind. But for many, though they may genuinely desire to forgive or believe they have forgiven, the hurt feelings attached, the trauma connected, the pain lying suppressed; is what needs to be released, evacuated, dealt with. *The main power of this therapy is to do just that.*

4. Invariably during the very first step of the therapy depending upon how deeply and sincerely you do it with feeling, you may break out in tears, sobs. This could last a long time, which in itself is the process of evacuation. Tears could be experienced at any stage of the Therapy. Another fallacy is to believe that becoming emotional, *crying and shedding tears is a sign of weakness.*

Obstacles:

1. The Therapy is so simple that the "thinker" or "intellectual" will perhaps feel tremendously foolish doing it.

   Talking to imaginary people! Shaking an imaginary hand! Sometimes the simplest solutions are the most effective.

2. One might be liable to believe that only the most complicated, most sophisticated and expensive treatments can bring about solutions. Hence when faced with this therapy which has cost you only the price of the book, it cannot be for real.

The Forgiveness Therapy is a very simple aid. It assists us to empty out the hurts and feelings locked up within us, over the years. Especially in the case of those who out of fear perhaps, have never spoken out their hurt to anyone, not even their best friend. Speaking out is necessary. Speaking out is therapeutic. Speaking out is healing. Once again, tears are part of the healing. Do not quench them.

It is possible that some will find it difficult to face another imaginary figure and begin the talking process. It is possible that for some it might become purely mechanical where feelings are not involved at all. It is possible some might become hysterical. Here is where we realize the importance of having a good friend or a counselor with you while doing this therapy. It is good to have

234

someone by your side who will be able to understand what is happening and help you out when required. This is provided of course, you do not mind such a person knowing your deepest innermost secrets. This is provided also you are absolutely sure such a person will in no way capitalize on the skeletons that emerge from the cupboard.

Apart from the tears, you may feel some form of heaviness, or headache, or discomfort of sorts. But as you forgive more and more deeply, you will experience lightness, like a burden or a stone being rolled away.

You may also experience vomiting, aches and pains that move around to different parts of the body, shivering, excessive yawning and other phenomena.. If so, this is a sign that areas of the spirit and the spiritual, need to be worked upon. Strong prayer support would be a great help but this is not under the purview of this book. There are many other publications that deal with these areas.

Work Shop At every programme we conduct a workshop by inviting one to come forward to do the Forgiveness Therapy in front of the whole group. This becomes first hand field experience for all. Someone who will not implicate family in very specific ways, one who does not have anything too intimate, such as the sexual area, to reveal. This is not a time to exercise acting skills but real live therapy. This is the example of George, fifteen years old, just out of school.

Step I. Accusing in Love

Sitting in his chair and in his mind's eye seeing his father seated in the opposite chair.

"Daddy (with great hesitation and apprehension) for the first time in my life I am talking to you from my heart. Please listen to me. I have always been afraid of you. When you drink, you get drunk and our home becomes a hell. The whole day, while you are away, we feel relaxed and able to do our studies and house chores. We are happy when you are not there. But when you come home, there is silence, each one pretending to be engrossed in his/her work. We don't even lift our eyes to see where you are going and what you are doing, lest you spot us and hit us with your cane. We are all petrified and so is Mummy.

So many times and for no reason at all, you will shout at her, beat her in front of us, scream abusive words at her. Just like you treat us. It is all the same. For you, we are like animals. And yet you are the worst animal of all. You call us harlots and bastards. Are you a father and a husband? What kind of person are you? Where did you come from? Even the neighbours do not look at you.

That is not all. (And as George gets more and more into the therapy you can feel the fear and anger, expressed in his words. His face contorted with rage, his fists balling up. As you look at him, he is not merely play acting, but actually talking it out with his father, longing to hit him a good hard punch yet restrained because he is not yet big enough). Do you know how the neighbours look with scorn upon us and laugh when they see you all drunk? In school too, they all know about you and make fun of me.

Why should this happen to me? What have I done to you that you should behave like this? You never let me go out with my friends, you never allow me to watch my television programme, you make me do so many chores at home that I do not have time to do my studies. If I am home even one minute beyond seven o'clock you let me have it with your cane. When you hit, you use the full force of your strength. I can even now feel the cane cutting into my back and my legs. Stop it, stop it, damn you. (By this time, he is sobbing away, his hands over his head, cowering down, and you know he is going through the process of being whipped mercilessly).

(George cries out for fifteen long minutes before we can begin to calm him down a little).

Step II Accused asking forgiveness

George changes chairs and sits in his father's place, responding now to what he has just told his father. George speaks to himself, as though he is his father.

George my son, while I sit here listening to you, I can only say,

I do not know what comes over me when I drink. I do not know why I drink in the first place. Maybe it is because when I was your age, my father treated me in the same way. In fact, do you know he would be so vicious that he would strip me naked sometimes and throw me out of the house. I am sorry if I am allowing my past to be the cause of your pain today. I cannot help it. I don't want to do it but there seems a force inside me that pushes me. It is like a devil within me.

All I know is I mean the best for my family but I must be so deceived into all I do to you all. Please, please forgive me. I know you are only fifteen and I am forty-five. It is an unfair advantage I have taken of you. I have hurt you deeply. I want to love you and show you my concern."

Step III Forgiving and Loving:

Changing chairs again, George resumes his role as himself.

"Daddy I know you were not made like this by God, but you formed into this horrible person you have become, because of your own past. I know that deep within yourself you are truly a lovable person. And I want to help you become yourself by forgiving you. You will always be my father no matter what. And I will always be there for you. In God's name, I forgive you. And in His love, I love you. (repeating that over and over again, you can see George settling into a peace that was not there when he began).

This short 15 or twenty minute episode is insufficient to empty his heart of all that is lying within him. There will be other experiences, other moments of humiliation and fear, in his young life. Therefore, we encourage him to carry on with the Forgiveness Therapy by doing it again and again, whenever he feels. There is no hard and fast rule that you can do it only so many times. In fact there is no rule at all.

What about you, dear reader. If you are forty years of age, you have much ground to cover. Doing the Forgiveness Therapy as above for a mere fifteen minutes certainly cannot deal with your whole life's hurting and paining. You would certainly need to delve into it, remain quite a while in any given situation before it can be complete.

A short exercise

Take the age of a person as 30. Follow this equation below:

30 x 365 (days) x 24 (hours) x 60 (minutes) x 60 (seconds) = 946,080,000 moments of existence in that persons life. Now to this add the average length of time in the mother's womb, i.e., 9X30X24X60X60=23,328,000. Making it a gross total of 969,408,000. A person aged 30 has existed for so many seconds/moments.

Substitute the figure 30 for your own age and work out the total amount of time you have existed in this world. How many of these moments are hurting? If for example you have missed out on your father's love from early childhood, then all these moments of your life upto date, are still bereft, empty of your father's love. Think about it.

Example 45: Teresa

Teresa was unable to forgive her grandmother. Try as she did, using the forgiveness therapy, she knew she hadn't yet forgiven. Some years earlier her mother told her that when she was married to her father, her mother-in-law, i.e. Teresa's Grand-mother did not reveal to her the full extent of her father's illness. This lead to a number of problems all through the marriage and her mother as a consequence went through a lot of suffering and hardship.

Teresa blamed her grandmother for it all and though she was aware she needed to forgive was unable to arrive at that point of forgiveness. When analyzing it further I asked Theresa "How did you feel as a result of all this? Can you describe in a word or two what effect all of this has had upon you?"

"I feel cheated" she said, in a moment and without any hesitation.

"Do you remember a further root, a deeper cause as to when, how and why this feeling of being cheated might have begun?"

After some time of discussion and analysis, this is what resulted. Teresa's mother was first introduced to another boy by an aunt. This boy could have given her a much better life in every respect. For some unknown reason the aunt pulled out and stopped her from marrying the boy. This alone brought hurt and pain to her.

Later she was introduced to her present husband and married him. Soon after they were married, her mother came to realize that the man she had married had some hidden and unrevealed problems. Teresa's mother began to feel 'cheated'. She had been deprived of marrying the first boy who could have given her a much better life and was encouraged to marry the second boy, now her husband, without being told of all his problems.

The feeling of being 'cheated' began here. And it is from here, i.e. from the moment Teresa was conceived in her mother's womb that she was given these negative feelings of being cheated. It was in this atmosphere of feeling "cheated" by her mother's aunt, that she was conceived in her mother's womb. She had now to forgive her mother's aunt and her own mother too. For it was through her mother that she picked up these feelings of being cheated. After this, she was free to forgive her grandmother.

Some will find blocks of this nature, to forgiveness. The inability to reach that point of final release. This is a sign that something even deeper lies hidden and needs to be uncovered. Till that root is uncovered and forgiven, the person is somehow bound and unable to forgive.

Guilt Feelings

Thus far, we have dealt with hurt that we have received from others. In order to be healed of such hurt one needs to forgive those who have imparted that hurt to us. But there will also be occasions when we have hurt others, when we have wounded others with words and actions. In such cases too, we can use the forgiveness therapy, slightly altered.

In chapter nine, you were encouraged to correct the wrong done to others. Despite taking action of some kind, one might still feel guilty, or have guilt feelings about the same. You still need to feel and experience the forgiveness from those persons. You need to be assured that the persons you have hurt, have forgiven you. Here is where this slightly altered version of the Therapy can be used. And especially in the area of Abortion, it becomes very effective.

Example. You have emotionally and physically abused your wife, in a fit of anger and/or drunkenness.

This is more realistic and common than one would like to imagine. Since then you have apologized profusely, bought her flowers, taken her out to a candle light dinner; but in the quiet of the night you still feel guilty at what you had done. Use the therapy as follows.

Step I. Step II used in the earlier occasions, now actually becomes step I.

You imagine your spouse is opposite you and open your heart by asking forgiveness. Do this through a process of recalling, reliving, in detail and aloud. Express what you did, how you felt while you were doing it. Try to understand how it has affected her, humiliated her, frightened her, angered her. Your actions and words robbed her of her respect and her beauty.

Try to explain what triggered it off. Something that took place or that she said, triggered off something in your subconscious. If you understand the root, explain how the root is affecting you today and especially in what you have done to her. However whether you understand or not, you are taking full responsibility for the episode. Finally, you say "I am so sorry, please forgive me".

Step II. Step III in the original version now becomes step II.

Changing chairs, taking her place, imagining you yourself are seated opposite, you speak now for her. Let her say to you "I forgive you" as explained above. Her forgiveness also has to be unconditional and complete.

Step III. Changing chairs again, being yourself and imagining she is opposite you once again, audibly accept her forgiveness and thank her for it. Believe she has forgiven you. Believe the hurt is now in the past and over.

Not forgetting prayer, which can bring to completion the whole process.

Forgiveness Therapy with Aborted embryos/foetus'/ unborn child

The need and reason for using this therapy in the case of aborted children, has been explained at the end of Chapter nine. Hence the goal of the therapy is to recognize that embryo, that foetus, that child; to give it an identity; to make it feel respected and accepted, welcomed and important; to let it know it is a separate entity, with a special role to play in family, community and society.

And this is what must emerge in Step I described just above. The first and sure way of recognizing that child, is by giving it a name and a birthday. This provides an identity, an existence. Promising never to forget him/her, always to remember his/her birthday, brings further acceptance, acknowledgement and healing to that child. Telling it at this step, that he/she is part of the family, that the family is not complete without him/her, that the family miss that child, all adds to the recognition and healing process.

The mother/father, stand in for themselves, for others who may have encouraged or supported the abortion and on behalf of the whole family. They ask for forgiveness from that child. They could add:

"I/We ask you to release us from the burden of our guilt and shame. Release us from the curse of our sin and wrong-doing. Set us free from anything that still binds us to this sin of ours."

At *step II*, (now on behalf of that child), the child gives forgiveness to the whole family, thanking them for acknowledging, respecting and loving him/her as part of the family. The child also releases parents and family from the burden of their guilt by saying:

"I release you, I set you free. Go in God's name. Go in Jesus name. I love you".

Finally at *step III*, on behalf of the whole family, accept that forgiveness and healing.

Strangely, after such a programme, physical cures of long standing take place. Mysterious aches and pains tend to disappear. Peace descends upon a family, which until then experiences rebellion, disobedience and disunity. In extreme cases, even mentally ill patients seem to become normal.

The Forgiveness Therapy is an aid, a help, an exercise that assists in evacuating and emptying out our hurting hearts. There are no rules. No restrictions. No limitations. Nothing to say you can do it only so many times or you cannot do it more than so many times. The only requirement is that it ends with forgiveness. Forgiveness being the source to any healing, forgiveness is the key. The key that opens the door to the rest of your life. The door to healing and wholeness.

Forgiveness Therapy with those who have been extremely Dominating, Controlling, Strict, Overpossessive, Over protective, Overattached.

Understand that this person or persons have had an influence in your life, over and above the ordinary. Till date this undue influence still has effect upon your behaviour, addictions, attitudes, temper and such like. The said person may or may not be alive still. That is immaterial. Hence while at *Step I* of the therapy, after speaking out all the feelings and hurt, *be sure to ask said person to release you from his/her grip, to let go of you, to remove once and for all their undue influence or attachments that stunt your growth emotionally and spiritually, to give you permission to be free.* Again be detailed in what you want to say.

In *Step II* let said person follow your request by letting go of you, in words setting you free and allowing you to be the person you were meant to be, besides asking you for forgiveness.

In *Step III* while forgiving him, thank him for releasing you and setting you free. Believe it. Breathe in freely your release, your freedom.

Forgiveness Therapy with the Sexually Abused

I was aghast as I listened to the speaker share her experience of being raped and abused when a child. Sexual abuse and molestation is so common and spoken of without any inhibitions that I wonder if the effects have been played down.

On the other hand in India, women being more modest and traditional, would find it very painful and embarrassing to use terms denoting the sexual organs. The inability to speak out aloud words such as penis, vagina, buttocks, breasts, would itself keep her bound, in addition to the hurting experience.

Remember, you are doing the therapy alone, with no one else besides you. Make use of this opportunity to break free from these fetters, from narrow-mindedness, from fear, from shame.

Forgiveness Therapy for Loss of a loved one

Step I would comprise:

i) recalling and reliving friendships, closeness, happy times, dependence.

ii) Realizing that your life is so empty now but cannot let it remain this way

iii) *Letting go of loved one in more words than one, and asking the same of him/her. Looking forward to freer and happier times.*

Step II The accused lets go and in turn waves goodbye, asking forgiveness for leaving you empty and alone.

Step III You forgive, thanking him/her for releasing and letting go of you, in turn you release him/her.

Chapter Fifteen

A TESTIMONY

THE STORY OF ANTHONY AND CHRISTINA

Anthony was pointed out to Christina. Independently and unaware, she was pointed out to him. They had occasion to meet, fall in love, corresponded endlessly and finally married.

The first argument they had, was at an international airport while waiting for their connecting flight, a few days after they were married. It indicated the different view-points and opinions each had on a particular subject. Subsequently they had many more, sometimes due to their individual and personal influences, likes and dislikes. Often their arguments centered around a lack of proper communication. Each one believed the other communicated a certain belief or attitude, from tone of voice, words incorrectly interpreted, a shrug of the shoulders, extended silence.

These arguments would leave them spent, hearts torn apart, mentally exhausted and emotionally wounded; robbing them of peace and the beauty of their romance. However, the love that first brought them together, enabled them to thrash out the differences and communicate to their heart's content, if necessary until the early hours of the morning. Finally, understanding and forgiving, peace returned to their hearts.

In lighter and happier moments, Christina would sometimes joke: "Well, I am the eldest in my family and used to telling everybody what to do, whereas you are among the youngest and used to doing whatever everybody has to tell you. So you better listen to me now!" Not withstanding the fact that age-wise, she is ten years his junior!

Let us attempt to understand their individual backgrounds.

ANTHONY

I am a product of a God-fearing, united and loving family. My father worked hard to support the family with dignity and grace. I am seventh in line among eight brothers and sisters. Using the chart in chapter 10, the following is my position in the family, marked in bold.

Dad

G B B B G B 2 yrs. 4 months ⑧ 6 yrs. 3 months G

Mum

My brother, elder to me by two years is named Benjamin, after the youngest of the sons of Jacob, an important character in the Bible. This was jokingly spoken of by our father, on occasion. I remember very clearly a visitor of yesteryears asking my father why my elder brother was named Benjamin and not myself. His answer was very clear – "He was supposed to be the last in the family".

Consequently when I did come along, it would have been an unexpected surprise for my parents. With all the love in their hearts they would have worked at accepting me and loving me as I was/am. Till that happened, which could be any time in the womb or even after birth, I would have experienced a certain lack of acceptance and rejection, deep in my unconscious. Perhaps I felt I had come at the wrong time, an extra, a mistake.

For six years I was the baby of the family, having my mother's lap exclusively to myself. I received much tender love and affection. But I was caught between my elder brother and my younger sister.

Elder to me by 2 years and more, Benjamin is a gem of a man, having a wonderful family of his own. But in his younger days, he came across to me as a bully, dominating and controlling. Perhaps this was because he himself was fighting to find himself. The sister before him was the beautiful one, the pet of our father's eye. His brother after him, i.e., myself, replaced him on mother's lap, when he was barely two years old. He felt like the bone in the middle.

Six years later came my sister who ousted me from my parents love and attention, the position I had got so used to. Subconsciously, I would have felt neglected and unloved. Perhaps that is the reason for the sibling rivalry with my sister, for no apparent conscious understanding or reason.

One mode of neglect and rejection, added upon another, deepens and strengthens the idea of being unwanted. Domination brings fear and timidity. I grew up timid, insecure, lacking confidence in myself.

To add icing to the cake, when I was barely 12 ½ yrs old, I contracted what was diagnosed as a rare, galloping cancer of the knee bone. An operation to amputate the leg was necessitated before it could spread further. Obviously this added to my insecurity, timidity, anxiety about the future, lack of confidence; all resulting in a poor self-image.

With this background, I met and married Christina. No doubt the healing process had begun much before we even met, but much was still left to be accomplished by the time we married.

CHRISTINA

Due to financial responsibilities, both being the eldest in their respective families, my parents married late in life. They too, worked very hard to provide their children facilities, which most others were not able to enjoy. We were trained to help out with the various chores in the house and grew to be a talented, united and praying family.

I am the eldest in our family of four sisters and a brother. It was in this atmosphere of financial challenges that I was conceived. Dad was ever so eager to have a son as his first child and kept a swanking new toy fire engine for him. As luck would have it I did not turn out to be that boy. When mum presented me to him, her words were "I am sorry I have disappointed you".

This is the beginning of my history of hurt, rejection, rebellion.

Other sisters came in quick succession, which added to the rejection. As a young girl I was put in charge of the others while Dad and Mum were away at work. In my impatience with them I would reprimand and correct them often. Complaints thus went back to mum and dad who would chastise me.

This is how my subconscious must have "reasoned". "As it is you have given me reason to feel unwanted. You are not making life any easier for me when you put me in charge of the others and then chastise me for using my authority wrongly. You give me added reason to feel rejected."

Independent and used to working things out for myself, with a strong mind and self-confidence in most areas, and yet a glaring lack of confidence in others; uninterested in household chores such as shopping, cooking, cleaning; I met and married the only man I fell in love with.

Anthony and Christina, each with their unique backgrounds, made a decision to commit, love and give of themselves to one another. Fortunately, independently and together, they began working upon the shortcomings which they brought into the Marriage. With the above very basic analysis, they are able to help, strengthen and support one another.

The motive and objective to the above analysis is not to point a finger at parents and others. Once that begins, there can be no hope of any healing and change. But as any medical practitioner might need to make a diagnosis of his patients condition, in order to treat, the same principle has to be followed here. The purpose is to diagnose what can be called the ROOT hurt or cause of one's malady.

Today, each has denied themselves and given up much for the other. They feel empty and incomplete without the other. Happiness, joy and success of life is not in their individual accomplishments and successes, but strangely in and through the other. Christina is consciously proud of her husband and grows ever more beautiful as he encourages her in the use of her gifts and talents. Though he is unable to do any fancy steps on the dance floor, she does not perceive him as handicapped. Anthony loves to

247

show his wife off! Forgetful but unconcerned he has often introduced or presented her more than once!

And surely this is not unique only to them. Many others have had much more experience in marriage than these two; have gone through life's challenges with each other and can boast of even sixty years of marital bliss. But this can never happen without a commitment to love, a commitment to giving of self to one another.

Other inter-related issues have a knack of popping up every now and then and this process of healing the hurts, continues. Healing life's hurts becomes a life long process. If you have by this stage begun upon yourself, you have only begun to scrape the tip of the iceberg.

Christina

Ever since I have known Christina, she has had a phobia, a fear at the sight of blood. Years earlier at a hospital where her father was to undergo some treatment, she was shown around the Kidney Dialysis Department where, at the sight of the blood passing through the tubes, she swooned and almost fainted. More recently with our three boys, the boys being what they are; scratches, bruises, scars and finally stitches being part of the daily routine, the sight of blood would make her squirm within herself. Finally one day, she offered to donate blood for a needy cause. Normally within twenty minutes the bottle ought to have filled, but it was more than half an hour and there was not much to show for the effort. Her palms had become clammy, her hands icy cold. The nurses decided to call it a day.

Later that day while recounting this incident to me, she confessed that while she did not feel any fear whatsoever consciously, she did experience the symptoms of fear i.e., feeling cold and clammy. This was a clear indication of something deeper and unresolved, something that went even further back into her life. It pointed to the time when as a little girl along with her sisters she would spend the evenings at a nearby park. A regular visitor to the park was a local magician who would entertain them with his tricks. Among them was the ill-famous one of swallowing blades and removing them unscathed. On this particular occasion he misfired, the blades stuck and all Christina remembers was seeing him lie in a pool of blood. She and her sisters were quickly whisked away to safer pastures but the unfortunate incident remained embedded in her memory.

We can learn two important lessons from this experience. One already mentioned above that sometimes a hurt can be so deeply embedded into the subconscious that we cut off from the negative feelings connected to those hurts. We experience the signs but not the feelings.

The second lesson we learn is that we can have many such experiences of fear or whatever, each one piling one upon the other over the days and years. Each one needs to be dealt with but there is always the first initial fear lying at the base which when revealed and dealt with, brings about a total change of personality. That is the time when the fear first hit and left its mark, left a dent, left a raw and vulnerable spot in that area of the psychology of the person. That spot can be called the ROOT. It is this root that needs to be discovered and dealt with in order to experience change and a healing.

Dealing with the root hurts of rejection as described earlier, even saw a physical healing in her menstrual cycles. Due to rejection, her subconscious was trying in some way to compel her to be the boy that her father had so much longed for. By being that boy, he would be happy and she would be more accepted and healed. But boys do not have periods and menstrual cycles. Thus as a young girl she has had irregularities, and often no menstruation for as much as six months at a stretch.

However as she worked on her root hurts through forgiveness and accepting herself for who she is, things have been restored to normal. Absolute normalcy.

Anthony

My very first experience of emotional healing took place at a large gathering of people for a religious convention. I was led to the counsellor, a religious nun, to whom I said – "What use is this life of mine with one leg. Where can I go, what can I accomplish. What hope is there for me."

Her answer to me was – You work upon yourself, i.e., the healing of your past hurts, and you will automatically get to know what the future has in store for you. Having quizzed me on my childhood hurts she led me through a little exercise to forgive my brother for his domination over me. Little did I realize at that moment, what an impact that little exercise would have upon me. The convention ended and we parted company.

Three weeks later one morning, I awoke with a sudden realization that I was healed of a terrible ailment that had been pricking me like a thorn in the flesh, until then. What I surmised then, due to a combination of factors such as rejection, my brothers loving domination, my amputation; I had developed an unnatural attraction to little boys, ever since my teen years.

In my attempts to live a sincere Christian life, this was the one thorn that dug a deep hole inside me. Even when a teen, I had quietly, without my parents knowledge, consulted a psychiatrist. The only result of those consultations was my pockets would be emptied of what little I had. I felt guilty as hell. Knowing from the Bible and Christian teaching, that it was not right, many a time in prayer I would cry out for mercy. This weakness of mine was like a sword of Damocles over my head. I consulted Catholic Priests for help. They gave me advice but no healing seemed to come my way.

You can therefore understand my ecstatic joy when I awoke that morning to realize that for those three weeks since I was counseled and prayed with, my unnatural tendency towards little boys had vanished into thin air. I felt like Archimedes, who when he discovered the principal of buoyancy, ran down the street naked. I was so overwhelmed with joy and gratitude that I could have jumped over my second floor balcony and run down the street shouting, 'I am healed, I am healed'.

The strange thing is I had not, in shame, told the counselor this part of my story. After all, she was a woman. Yet the greatest healing that could ever happen, took place in my life, without realizing it, at that moment. This led to other areas and moments of healing.

You already know that at the age of 12 ½ I contracted a rare and galloping cancer of the right knee. My limb had to be amputated. Much later, involved with the local community, church and friends, bustling around like any busybody, up and down the stairs and all around town on my three-wheeler scooter, many drew inspiration from me, my charming smile and helpful ways. When told that my operation must have been a terrible trauma for me, my response would be: 'Oh yes, but I have long since got over that', implying I had recovered and was totally healed.

However, one day, a relative who was for sometime residing with us, took ill and had to be hospitalized. As is the custom in the family, each one of us would take turns to spend the night and day with him. When my turn came, I remember being most uncomfortable in the hospital, hating the smell of ether (the disinfectant used to dress my wounds 16 years earlier), with this strong irrational desire to jump out of the fourth floor balcony of the hospital and run away. I had to make a conscious effort to control my urges and fears.

On the advice of my sister I spent time in quiet reflection, recalling my own operation at the age of 12½ and all the incidents that lead to it. I began a process of recalling (memory) and reliving (being aware of the negative feelings attached to the memories) the details and the persons involved or responsible for my condition. From the cycle accident when I grazed my knee badly, to the pain on walking, which developed a couple of weeks later; my inability to continue with school, my brother calling me a fusspot and a sham, the round of doctors, the round of tests, one thing leading to another and finally the bone biopsy which confirmed the cancerous growth.

As I followed each stage above, recalling details and

forgiving the person who caused the accident, my brother for teasing me, the doctors and nurses and my own parents for causing inconvenience, pain and tension. I experienced the flow of tears, at first a drop here and a drop there. Then came the actual day of the operation. I recollected the visitors in the room, the flowers all around, friends who kept me in splits of laughter while cheating at a game of cards in order to distract my attention. Till finally the nurse walked in and I knew the time had arrived. It was a sudden shock of fear as I remember bracing myself. With tense muscles I was wheeled out and into the operation theatre. I recollected the dim lights, the chill of the air conditioning, nurses busy with face-masks and the anesthetic defying me to count up to four. Consciously I was aware I managed to count only up to three and then it was lights out for me.

Not knowing what to do after that, I imagined leaving my body and watching the scene from way above. I imagined the Doctor making the first incision with his knife after which I was overwhelmed with tears. Till then remembering all the details and forgiving every single person concerned, was like a leaking tap with the tears forced out drop by drop. Now it was a tap opened to the full with the tears gushing out freely and fully. I cried for two hours non-stop, with what felt like electric currents traversing the length and breadth of my body. I realized later that this was the shock to the nervous system, the pain and the trauma of the operation that I was being relieved of. This was a new step, the beginning to the rest of my life.

Why was I always under the impression that I had overcome the trauma of my operation? Why was I never aware of the trauma and shock to my whole system? I realized then that I was under anesthesia during my operation. I was unconscious. Therefore the shock and trauma was totally in my unconscious and consciously I would never ever have woken up to this truth if it were not for the incident when the relative had to be hospitalized. Until this occasion, though deep within me I was insecure about my future, anxious and with a poor self-image; on the outside I never showed it for I looked and behaved like any normal person. But having dealt with this situation in my life, today I can truly say it brought about a great healing, a restoration of my self-confidence and a new avenue for my life.

A third major area of healing took place many years later. Strangely it was as a result of another young man, also physically handicapped, whom I was counselling. Mind you and, I repeat for purposes of emphasis, that I was counselling him. John tells me over the phone one day – "Anthony, it suddenly occurred to be this morning that you have not as yet forgiven God for taking away your leg through cancer".

I chuckled as I analysed what I believed to be true. It was in fact John who, as a result of a severe motor accident many years ago was left physically handicapped, robbed of a promising career, apart from opportunities to see the world. I felt he was now transferring his hurt and anger towards God, onto me.

As I proceeded to relate the incident to Christina, later in the day, I almost hit the roof at hearing her response – "Yes he is right". I could feel the anger boil within me. I could sense it rising, ready to be released like a volcano and it would have if I had not listened to a quiet voice which seemed to say to me – "Listen to what she has to say".

I listened. The work I was doing was wonderful and could not be compared with anything else. So many individuals, marriages, homes were beginning to live fuller and more meaningful lives. The word had reached far and wide and many more were interested in attending my programmes. The book itself and its contents is a sign of this wonderful work.

Yet I was not satisfied. I was not able to fully appreciate what was being done. The nature and importance of what I was doing did not provide contentment and peace. Instead I compared myself with other "successful" people. And what she spoke was the truth.

I spent many long hours in reflection, in analysis and in proceeding to further my healing. I took a long hard look at myself. Knowingly and with a conscious determination I accepted the way I was, the way I was always going to be. I aimed at being content with myself. I grew in the awareness and truth that despite my handicap, I was still special, I was still unique and always would be. No more need I feel insecure or inferior. No more need I prove myself to anyone or in any situation. In the process I was led to forgive once again, my parents, the medical profession and all others. This brought about a peace deep within me, I have never known before.

> *"We are not some casual
> and meaningless product of evolution.
> Each of us is the result of a thought of
> God.
> Each of us is willed, each of us is loved,
> each of us is necessary."*
>
> — Pope Benedict XVI